PENGUIN B

846

TEN YEARS UNDER THE EARTH

NORBERT CASTERET

TEN YEARS
UNDER THE EARTH

*

NORBERT CASTERET

PENGUIN BOOKS
HARMONDSWORTH · MIDDLESEX

Dix ans sous terre first published in France 1933
Au fond des gouffres first published in France 1936
Ten Years under the Earth first published 1939
Published in Penguin Books
by arrangement with J. M. Dent & Sons Ltd
London WC2
1952

*

Translated and edited by
BURROWS MASSEY

Made and printed in Great Britain
for Penguin Books Ltd
by Hunt, Barnard and Co, Ltd, Aylesbury
Collogravure Plates by Harrison and Sons Ltd

CONTENTS

*

PART FOUR
UNDER GROUND

PART FIVE
PUZZLES AND WONDERS BELOW GROUND

PART SIX
DISCOVERY OF THE TRUE SOURCE OF THE GARONNE

INTRODUCTION

In 1923 Norbert Casteret made his name by a master stroke, the discovery of the prehistoric drawings and statues in the cavern of Montespan (Haute-Garonne). He has uncovered many other caverns since.

It was, then, in the strange domain of prehistory that he won his first successes.

At Montespan he made his astonishing find by a piece of unparalleled daring: he plunged under a submerged ceiling into the shadows of an underground river, braving a tunnel whose length he could not know. As he neither drowned nor cracked his skull at the first attempt, the adventure whetted his appetite. This perilous feat is now one of his professional tools. It brought him to grips with the most difficult of scientific problems and with practical underground hydrogeology – the mysteries still surrounding abysses, caverns, subterranean reservoirs, and the like.

For more than ten years he has been busy discovering and exploring underground rivers like that of the Mas d'Azil (Ariège), which pierce the outlying ranges of the Pyrenees (e.g. the Plantaurel, the Petites Pyrénées). Every year Norbert Casteret adds to the list of those curious water-courses, only two or three of which were known at the beginning of the century; their astonishing multiplication begins to take on the character of a general law, sure before long to attract the attention of geologists.

In caverns at moderate altitudes Casteret has gathered proof that this order of phenomena is universally important.

At an altitude of some 8,800 feet he made another important discovery: an underground water-course behind the Cirque de Gavarnie, among the lapiaz and ice-filled caverns (Grotte Casteret) on the Spanish side of the Marboré. The Cascade de Gavarnie and the Torrent of Pau have their true origin here. Recently M. J. Devaux has even traced the stream underground to an elevation of 9,450 feet, under the three peaks of the Cascade.

Morphologists should find it interesting to compare this with the underground streams of Circassia, at from 6,500 to 7,800 feet (1903), and the Dachstein and the Eisriesenwelt at Salzburg (1909 *to* 1921); *they have as yet given the subject insufficient attention.*

Casteret spent four years, from 1928 *through* 1931, *in settling the controversy begun in* 1787 *over the communication (asserted by one party, and denied by the other) between the cavern of the Trou du Torn* (6,500 *feet), at the foot of the Maladetta, and the resurgence of the Goueil de Jouéou* (4,550 *feet), the chief source of the Garonne, in the Val d' Aran (Spain). Here his power of close and persistent reasoning came to his aid.*

He reached his conclusions by patient and masterly study; they were wholly confirmed by a sensational coloration test. Sixty kilograms of fluorescein, thrown into the abyss at eight p.m. on 19 *July* 1931, *coloured the Goueil on the* 20*th, before six a.m. — less than ten hours* (1,300 *feet per hour, a very rapid rate). The colouring did not wholly disappear for twenty-seven hours, and it went down the Garonne beyond Saint-Béat in France, more than thirty miles.*

It is therefore now established that the water from the eastern glaciers of the Maladetta (Pic d' Aneto) goes not to Spain by the Esera and the Ebro, but to France, by the Goueil and the Garonne. Its underground passage of 16,360 *feet of distance, and nearly* 1,950 *feet of height (whose subterranean cascades will perhaps be discovered some day), goes under the axis of the Pyrenees and the European watershed. This passage is much more impossible than that of the upper Danube, which reappears at Aach, on the Rhine slope.*

Since 1932 *Casteret has been studying a similar problem at the northern frontier of the Val d' Aran (Spain) and the department of Ariège. Do the waters received by the magnificent cavern of the Embudo de Liat reappear at the resurgence of Ardan (France), or of Arros (Spain)? . .*

This is 'real geography' indeed.

Three precious qualities make Casteret's work significant and successful: the daring (sometimes too great) with which he attacks obstacles that have stopped his predecessors (especially the dangerous 'siphons' or submerged tunnels); the order and method with which he plans his work and perseveres in a subject once begun; and finally the self-discipline which enables him to learn from and lean upon those who can teach him. It has always been a great pleasure to assist a man of such tact and good sense.

This book is the first phase, and a most fruitful one, in a career original, instructive, and useful. As Casteret goes on, he should bring us many surprises; already he belongs in the galaxy of great Pyreneists. He has made the subterranean Pyrenees his own, and this is a promising chapter in applied hydrogeology.

ÉDOUARD-ALFRED MARTEL

TRANSLATOR'S NOTE

THIS volume contains the essential parts of two successive books from M. Casteret's pen: *Dix ans sous terre*, which was honoured by the French Academy, and *Au fond des gouffres*. Fortunately nothing had to be omitted beyond some passages of chiefly local French interest. Chapters from the two volumes are interwoven in what seemed logical order, without attempt at segregation.

In translating I have clung rather to the spirit than to the letter of the narrative – an easy matter with so exciting a story; but I have taken every care to give the scientific passages their full value. Measurements are converted from the metric system with whatever exactness the context requires; in the Pyrenean nomenclature I have tried (perhaps without perfect success) to apply French names to French peaks, and Spanish names to Spanish peaks. The author, true son of the Pyrenees, probably thinks of them all in his native dialect.

M. Casteret has brought up to date for the English edition one or two matters which were still in doubt when the French books appeared.

B. M.

FOREWORD

I KNOW and love caverns, abysses, and subterranean rivers. Studying and exploring them has been my passion for years. Where can one find such excitement, see such strange sights, enjoy such intellectual satisfactions as in exploration below ground?

Too many people think caverns are uniformly monotonous and uninteresting. 'Nothing but wet, blackness, and mud,' they say. This idea is entirely one-sided and incorrect. I do not think I have ever seen two grottoes alike. There is room for unlimited observation. Underground exploration requires unexpected talents – from prehistory, mineralogy, natural history, physics, and chemistry to rope acrobatics, crawling, canoeing, swimming, and even skating.

I have ventured to deal with prehistory only because I have discovered remains dating from the dawn of man and the extinct great animals. Geology too is an infinitely complex and poetic science, and I have been content to skirt its fringes, discussing what few aspects I have dabbled in.

My hand is more skilful with pick and rope than with the pen; but my familiarity with underground solitudes worthy of Dante must be my justification for writing this book. I lived it intensely long before I could write it.

I am afraid that words will be powerless to convey my impressions, to describe the indescribable. And I am afraid too that I have mentioned myself too often; but how do otherwise in telling of solitary adventure?

I have not tried here to describe the 500 caverns and underground water-courses which I have explored to date. I have confined myself to certain explorations that have opened new worlds below ground and new horizons to prehistory, geology, and geography. I have tried also to describe and explain certain subterranean puzzles and marvels which help make the science of caves, or spelaeology, a much more varied and fascinating branch of knowledge than is commonly known.

I cannot prove that my passion for caverns is a vague and

infinitely distant nostalgia for vanished aeons when men lived in caves. Yet who shall say that some sort of atavism does not play a part in this love of solitude and mystery? One can never really enjoy them to the full except underground.

Almost as influential as my natural penchant was a marvellous book, which impressed and fascinated me more than any other – Jules Verne's *Journey to the Centre of the Earth*. I have re-read it many times, and I confess I sometimes re-read it still, each time finding anew the joys and enthusiasm of my childhood.

*

My cave-haunting soon brought the study of prehistory in its train, and later that of geology and subterranean hydrology. The museum at Toulouse was a revelation. Many are the Thursdays and Sundays I have spent before the glass cases in the hall of caves, dreaming of the endless streams of centuries brought to life by the stone-age tools.

Courses taught by the archaeologist Cartailhac and his successor, Count Begouen, and the kindly and precious friendship of the distinguished historian Camille Jullian and the explorer and geologist É.-A. Martel encouraged me in studies which I had already begun by myself.

Then the War intervened. At eighteen I began the hard life of the trenches.

Returning safe from the War, I enthusiastically resumed my studies. My mind was now matured under fire, my body schooled to hardship and ready for the risks I was sure to encounter. No one can venture underground without agility and physical stamina, and these qualifications I possessed as a champion runner, jumper, and swimmer.

Thus, after four years' absence, I came back to my native Pyrenees. I spent all my leisure in exploring their caverns. From time to time they gave up some of their secrets, as this book will tell.

Sometimes – too seldom to suit them or me – I had the help of three loved ones whom I can never thank enough for their devoted labours: Dr Martial Casteret, my youngest brother, who nearly lost his life in a daring climb on the northern slope of the Col du Toro; and my mother and my wife, both mountaineers by instinct, high-spirited and indomitable in the face of fatigues and perils. Fortunate the explorer with such companions!

N. C.

PART ONE

AGES VANISHED IN THE NIGHT

*

Mystery is one of the greatest charms of nature
COUNT RUSSEL, *Souvenirs d'un montagnard*

I

THE OLDEST STATUES IN THE WORLD

*

The secret of all discoverers is that they regard
nothing as impossible
GUSTAVE LE BON, *Evolution de la matière*

*

In August 1922, my explorations in the Pyrenees brought me to the village of Montespan, on the slope of a hill crowned by a feudal castle. The ruins, dominating the Garonne, draw the eye from afar. They go back to the Lords of Montespan, who ruled there for centuries before the celebrated Mme de Montespan conquered the heart of the Sun King. Near the castle is the Grotte de Montespan, which this chapter is about.

After a visit to the ruins, I headed for the mouth of a supposedly impenetrable cavern in the neighbouring mountain. At the base of the mountain I found a crack in the rock, with running water coming out. The villagers claimed that in exceptionally dry summers one could wade into a natural corridor, but that after sixty-five yards the grotto ended, the ceiling dipping into the water.

This description I found correct. Undressing, and slipping through a hole the size of a man's body, I got into a horizontal gallery from ten to thirteen feet wide, and six to ten feet high.

I was wading in running water on a sand and clay bottom.

One hundred and thirteen feet in, the gallery made a right-angled turn; a sudden dip of the ceiling forced me to stoop far over. After twenty yards of this uncomfortable locomotion the water deepened, and the ceiling touched the surface.

This was an uneasy and discouraging stopping-place. But memories of previous explorations elsewhere reinforced my habitual obstinacy. Instead of leaving immediately, as was natural, I stopped in my strange posture to reflect.

The limestone rock around me indicated that this stream might have hollowed out caverns in the mountain. On the other hand, geology tells us that the climate at the end of the glacial epoch was cold and dry, rather like modern Lapland. If the cavern did exist, it would have been dry for a long time in the early quaternary era, and so might have sheltered the wretched prehistoric cave-dwellers.

Uncertain as it was, this theory appealed irresistibly to a prehistorian. I decided to dare the underground river, and push into the bowels of the mountain.

Neck-deep in the water as I was, I nevertheless considered the rashness of persevering alone in so hazardous an undertaking. Several possibilities came to mind: I might find the water bathing the ceiling ahead indefinitely, run into a cul-de-sac, get to a pocket of foul air, fall down a shaft, be entangled in branches carried down by the stream, or possibly go down in a quicksand. . . . After weighing these various chances in the awful silence and loneliness, I still decided if possible to force the barrier, impregnable though it seemed.

Putting my candle on a projection of the wall, I inhaled air for an immersion of two minutes (to me a familiar procedure). Then I plunged, one hand ahead, the other touching the ceiling. I felt the bumps and contours of the ceiling with infinite care; I was blind, with finger-tips for eyes. I had not only to go ahead, but to think about getting back. Suddenly, as I was going forward in this fashion, my head emerged; I could breathe.

There was no telling where I was; the darkness was complete. Obviously I had forced a siphon, a tunnel with a sub-

merged ceiling. I turned tail at once, and plunged in the opposite direction, for in such circumstances nothing is more
dangerous than to lose one's sense of direction. Below the
siphon I found my candle still mirrored in the black water.
Despite the slender and purely sporting result of this first
attempt, I was already anticipating the excitement of a second
expedition, which I hoped would be long and fruitful.

The following day I was back at the entrance to the grotto,
this time with an outfit both light and simple. Entirely undressing as before, and hiding my clothes in the bushes, I
slipped into the underground stream. I had a lighted candle in
one hand, and my rubber bathing cap full of matches and spare
candles in the other. This simple container, kept tightly closed,
would enable me to relight my candle after each dive or after
one of my numerous tumbles into the water.

At the siphon I took the precaution of steering in exactly
the same direction as I had before, so as to find the air pocket.
I came up safely with my eyes and nose just out of water. I
shook my dripping bathing cap to dry it before lighting a
candle; my caution was equal to my impatience. The flickering
light reached but a few yards; it showed me the ceiling parallel
to the water, with only a thin air-space between.

I went on, hugging the slightest unevenness in the rock
with my head, so as to get space to breathe. After a hundred
yards I reached a clay bank at the entrance to a vast chamber;
here I could recover somewhat from my excitement, but not
from the freezing cold.

The ceiling rose to a height of thirty-five or forty feet, and
the stream was half buried under great blocks fallen from
above. The hall was adorned with beautiful stalagmite cascades. I crossed it, and started wading again.

Familiar though I was with difficult caverns, I had never
known such a feeling of isolation, oppression, and terror. (The
most commonplace accident, such as losing or wetting the
matches, may always be fatal anywhere underground.)

Having got past an enormous pillar which rises from the
brook-bed, I was faced with a new and deadly looking siphon.
The water was deep, and the ceiling spiked with black, needle-

pointed stalactites. Repeating a manoeuvre already familiar but none the less breath-taking, I dived through this siphon as well. It seemed perceptibly longer than the first. I was now locked in the bosom of the shades by a double barrier. The loneliness was tremendous; I struggled against an uneasiness slowly turning to anguish.

Luckily the spot where I momentarily considered retreating was unsuited to even the briefest reflexion. Harried by cold and apprehension, I found I might as well go on as go back. I had to crawl for some distance in the water, in a small gallery whose low ceiling sent down a veritable shower which kept putting out my candle. This crawling was made the more arduous by constant bumping and scraping against the rough stone. Finally it brought me to a hall much vaster than the first, where an indescribable chaos of huge blocks testified to some past upheaval.

At this point I had to do frantic gymnastics to get back the circulation in my limbs, numbed by the glacial water.

My guess about the underground river had been amply confirmed; now I began to wonder how far the succession of corridors and chambers would take me. The water flowed endlessly, now smooth and silent, now murmuring noisily as it shot down little spillways.

First making sure of my candle supply, I scrambled on across piled-up blocks. I made my way out of the hall with some difficulty, and returned to the water in a long, monotonous gallery. At various narrow places, where I had to wriggle between limestone columns, I thought I had reached the end of the grotto; but always my feeble light opened further perspectives. I walked sometimes in the water, sometimes on slippery, sticky clay banks, where I left my footprints as precious signposts for the return.

I had long since lost all notion of time and distance when I was stopped by the narrowness of the corridor. For the previous few moments I had been literally crawling, with the greatest difficulty; the ceiling almost touched the water.

I had been struggling for hours to reach the end of the cavern; and here was an impassable bottle-neck halting me

without hope of finding the source. Fortunately my disappoint-
ment lasted but a moment. Having thrust my head and one
arm into the outlet, I gave a shout of triumph which put to
flight the mysterious occupants of a pool filled with mud and
branches – a colony of tadpoles, disturbed for the first time,
told me that the underground brook had quitted daylight,
fields, and woods, to plunge into the mountain but a few
yards upstream.

The presence of the tadpoles in this inaccessible spot was a
sure sign of open air close by; these creatures never venture
far into underground waters. I discovered in the next few days
that the disappearance of the brook was but a few yards off,
through an absolutely impassable rock fissure.

Although I had penetrated the mountain from side to side, I
had no choice but to go back the way I had come. This I
accomplished with increasing exhaustion, but without incident
beyond some agonizing doubts of direction at forks in the
cavern. I passed the worst of the two siphons only on my
second attempt, having dived at too great an angle the first
time.

I had entered the cavern in broad daylight, under a hot sun;
I came out chilled to the bone, with night upon me. I had
taken five hours to cover about a mile and seven-eighths, as
we found later when we measured.

Step by step I made further expeditions through the cavern,
inspecting new halls, an upper level, and a maze of low
galleries. I kept hoping to find some trace of prehistoric
habitation, which I thought rather probable from the period
when the cavern was dry. But a rainy spell unfortunately
swelled the brook, and shut off the cavern, so I had to put off
my investigations to the following year. Except in August and
September, the ceilings are submerged for stretches too long
to be swum.

My booty from the brook in 1922 was limited to one bison
tooth. But this discovery confirmed my opinion that the
cavern had been frequented by primitive man, and I waited
impatiently for the next dry season to go on with my search.

A year later I returned. This time I brought along a friend,

Henri Godin, a great swimmer and lover of underground expeditions. The summer of 1923 was unusually dry, and the water lower than it had been the year before. The roof of the first siphon, a flat arch, was not wholly submerged; the top of the arch was a couple of inches out of the water. We were able to have our eyes but not our mouths above water, and to keep our candles lit.

Godin had just come back from visiting the Grotte de Han in Belgium and the Gouffre de Padirac; he assured me, with chattering teeth, that the novelty of our aquatic excursion more than made up for the attractions of those celebrated caves.

We went on as far as an enormous pillar rising from the water, which seems to bid the visitor go no farther. A few yards beyond is the second siphon, which I had forced with such difficulty the year before, and which gives access to five-eighths of a mile more of underground water-course. Abandoning the arctic caresses of the brook, we entered a dry gallery 650 feet long.

This gallery, never more than sixteen feet wide by thirteen high, looks magical at first sight. The walls and ceiling are covered with limestone ridges and glittering stalactites. The floor is a succession of hollows whose waved and fluted edges make a natural staircase. Each tread is filled with clear water. Beyond, a bulging and granular floor of lovely yellow recalls the madrepore coral of submarine landscapes. But the luxuriance of form and colour comes to a sudden end. Beyond a sharp bend is a dark gallery of bare rock, its floor covered with soil.

We went down the corridor in Indian file; there was no sound but the slap of our bare feet on the clay. We had to cover the last hundred feet flat on our stomachs, between a misshapen ceiling and a cold, muddy floor. Retracing our steps, we came to a place where we could almost stand upright. Here, in an enlargement of the gallery, I chose a nook which looked promising for probing.

I attacked the solid clay with a portable tool which I carry on my explorations. My companion viewed me with a disappointed eye, wondering whether my sudden enthusiasm for excavation would keep us long in this unattractive retreat. After each blow of the pick I had to scrape off the sticky clay.

Suddenly my hand gripped a hard object, and even before I had freed it from the surrounding gangue (earth or stony matter in a mineral deposit), I knew I held one of those chipped flints which sometimes make the layman smile, but which delight any archaeologist. This simple flint, barely formed, but indubitably chipped and used, did in fact prove that primitive man had frequented the cavern. Small as the find was, it started a long train of thought, and more than ever I was struck by the resemblance between the grotto of Montespan and other Pyrenean caves rich in traces of the past.

It is a fact established in prehistory that primitive man lived in small grottoes or in the vestibules of the great caverns, but that he avoided the mazes deeper underground because of the darkness and the fear of wild beasts. And yet it has long been known that with very rare exceptions all prehistoric engravings and paintings occur in remote and inaccessible parts of the caverns. Evidently this is the result of a magical or religious rite which compelled primitive artists to create their strange works far from daylight and profane eyes.

This was why the finding of a chipped flint hundreds of yards underground seemed so important. The moment I found this proof that primitive man had been in the gallery, I stood up to search the walls by candle-light for the rock engravings which I thought must be there.

Meanwhile Godin, interested by now, had possessed himself of the pick, and was going on digging. Suddenly I stopped. Before me was a clay statue of a bear, which the inadequate light had thus far hidden from me (in a large grotto a candle is but a glow-worm in the inky gloom). I was moved as I have seldom been moved before or since. Here I saw, unchanged by the march of aeons, a piece of sculpture which distinguished scientists of all countries have since recognized as the oldest statue in the world.

My companion crawled over at my call, but his less practised eye saw only a shapeless chunk where I indicated the form of the animal. One after another, as I discovered them around us, I showed him horses in relief, two big clay lions, many engravings.

That convinced him, and for more than an hour discovery followed discovery. On all sides we found animals, designs, mysterious symbols, all the awe-inspiring and portentous trappings of ages before the dawn of history.

In the mud-stained notebook which I often carry underground, the grotto of Montespan is listed in 1922 under the serial number sixty-three. At the end of a few lines devoted to it after my first trip through the mountain, I had written the words: 'What has this grotto in store for me?'

Now, a year later, the morning after the discovery the press shouted the news. Then came archaeologists, French and foreign scientists, reporters and photographers. Their cars stopped at the little village of Montespan, which was much surprised at the sudden stir. After this followed official confirmation – classification of the cavern among historic monuments, awards from learned societies, felicitations from the Institut, among others, and the large gold medal of the Académie des Sports. The last was unexpected enough, but a satisfaction to one who sees no conflict between intellectual and physical culture.

The hitherto obscure archaeologist who had passed in the neighbourhood for a lunatic and a treasure-seeker, bore up under his notoriety as best he could. When at last quiet was restored, he pasted in his old notebook, below the previous year's question, 'What has this grotto in store for me?', a photograph from a magazine, bearing the caption: 'The Oldest Statues in the World.'

Immediately after the discovery the schoolmaster of a neighbouring village, eager to see the relics, but not anxious to tackle the siphon, dug a drainage channel at the entrance of the cavern in order to increase the flow of the brook and lower its level. Three days' further work by my brother Martial, my friends Dupeyron and Godin, and M. l'Abbé Moura, curé of Montespan, produced an air-space of about sixteen inches between water and ceiling, so that one could go through without diving or getting a mouthful; only a purifying bath was necessary in order to reach the prehistoric sanctuary. This preliminary work made the cavern accessible to scientists. Braving the cold water, they accompanied me in the most varied and sometimes abbreviated costumes through the pre-historic gallery.

The rock engravings and clay statues are from the beginning of the Magdalenian era; they date back, according to scientific-ally authenticated chronologies, about 20,000 years. There are fifty pictures of various animals (some species extinct or emigrated), deeply incised in the walls by means of flint gravers. The clay modelling is represented by thirty specimens, from real statues forty inches high down to little high-reliefs swallowed by the drip. These sculptures are the most import-ant part of the find, for the two clay bison statuettes found in 1913 by Count Begouen and his sons in the Ariège cavern of the Tuc d'Audoubert had been the sole examples known of prehistoric modelling.

I have mentioned the influence of certain caves visited before I attacked Montespan. The magnificent Pyrenean cavern of the Tuc d'Audoubert was one of those which impressed and educated me most. A trip through it involves canoeing along a subterranean river, climbing by ladders, and crawling through low corridors. This cavern taught me the minute and delicate task of looking for traces invisible to the unschooled observer.

The analogy between Montespan and the Tuc d'Audoubert is striking; but is it not remarkable for their similarity to go so far that these two caverns are the only ones yet known to con-tain clay statues?

Leaving the water at the great column, we came to the vestibule where the long procession of Magdalenian relics begins. The most important large animals of that epoch are engraved in the rock: the mammoth, the horse, the bison, the stag, the dziggetai (*Equus hemionus*, a relative of the donkey), the wild goat, the chamois, the hyena.

All these animals are drawn with the skill and striking

alism which one usually finds in the works of prehistoric man; his adeptness at animal portraiture was astounding.

Certain details are striking in their originality; others interest us because the artist's intention is so puzzling. For instance, one of the horses bears a right hand with outspread fingers, deeply engraved on its shoulder. Another horse was engraved with a rocky ledge as a natural spine, while an expressive chamois head is drawn around an oval pebble (part of the pudding-stone rock), forming the animal's eye.

Two horses' heads, face to face, are so different that there can be no doubt of the artist's intent to show different varieties. One of them has a massive head, prominent lips, dilated nostrils, and encroaching mane and beard, while the other has a fine, slender head, no beard, and a thin mane. Several of the animals' bodies show wounds, arrows, and unknown symbols. One of the bison has an oval design on its neck, and a dziggetai has on its rump a sharp V.

A hyena engraved on the ceiling of the passage which ends the gallery, a spot to be reached only by crawling, measures but two inches in length. I believe this is the smallest rock engraving ever found.

Finally I discovered among this collection of animals contemporary with the cave man a curious human profile with a round head, large nose, enormous round eye, and short beard.

Interesting as these designs are, the chief attraction of the Montespan cavern of course is the clay sculpture. Large chunks of clay clutter the floor at one of the turns in the long gallery; these are fragments of partly collapsed statues, which lean against a sloping wall.

These statues, three in number, are in Indian file. The first, a large feline sixty-seven inches long by twenty-eight inches high, seems to walk towards the entrance. Powerfully modelled in high relief to a thickness of sixteen inches, the raw and plastic clay of which it is moulded has partially collapsed of its own weight. The chunks thus detached and lying on the ground still show the contours of the animal; the head in particular has rolled between the forepaws, but it is hardly recognizable, although its outline still shows on the wall. The neck, chest, shoulders, and forelegs are in place; the hind quarters have collapsed, but as in the case of the head one can follow the contour on the wall, where one rear paw and the end of the tail still adhere.

The preserved parts and the general silhouette make the statue recognizable as a feline: the legs are powerful, the knees low, the chest compact, the body elongated. One last feature, the tuft of hair at the end of the tail, permits exact identification: this is a lion. Following this lion are two others, also standing and going in the same direction, but they are in even worse condition than the first.

The above imperfect description gives but a poor idea of the group, and can never take the place of actual inspection. The sculptures would not be worthy of further space if they were not almost unique in the world, and if they did not have certain conspicuous peculiarities of prime scientific interest.

The neck and chest of the first lion are literally riddled with lance- or javelin-marks. One wonders whether the statue and those that follow were not partly destroyed in that way. I shall explain these mutilations later; there are other examples in the cavern.

Continuing along the gallery, we reach an opening, the small low-ceiled chamber where my first probing yielded the chipped flint. This enlargement of the corridor, now called the 'Hall of the Bear,' is the most interesting part of the cavern.

Within a radius of thirty-odd feet is a whole museum of prehistoric sculptures. The most important statue is a headless bear. The bear, crouched in the posture of the Great Sphinx of Gizeh, is forty-three inches long by twenty-three and a half inches high. Like the lions it faces the entrance, but instead of leaning against the wall it sits about a yard away, on a small platform built for the purpose.

The statue is massive, as befits the animal it represents; its powerful hind quarters are well rounded, the hind paws are hidden under the belly, the right forepaw is outstretched, its five claws clearly indicated; the distinctive bear hump at the shoulders is very prominent. The animal apparently never had a head, for the cut of the neck is covered with patina like the rest of the body. Unlike the neck of the lion, it shows no signs of breakage.

The bear too, was the victim of many mutilations; it is riddled with round holes as of javelins forcefully hurled at the vital parts. But thanks to its solidity and its large base it resisted, and the body remains whole.

The drip from the ceiling has trickled down rump and flanks without damaging them, armouring some parts with a hard calcite film which proves the statue's antiquity beyond doubt. The skull of a bear-cub, of a size proportionate to the figure, lies between its forepaws. The skull was fixed to the statue by a wooden peg, and fell off when the peg disintegrated with time and damp. Traces of the peg are still visible.

Originally, then, the bear of Montespan was a clay statue with a real, gory head. We shall see later the probable meaning of this extraordinary combination; the frightful ceremonies which took place there in the bosom of the rock are almost nightmarish to imagine.

Three feet behind the bear a horse is deeply scratched in the clay floor. Its shoulder bears enigmatic signs, and it seems to have a tremendous flowing mane. The whole floor of the Hall of the Bear is embossed with thirty high-reliefs, twelve to twenty inches long by four to six inches thick. Unfortunately these sculptures have largely been eaten away by the water which has trickled through this part of the gallery. Most of them are disfigured, but some, out of reach of the water, show this to be a herd of horses; many of these, too, bear indecipherable symbols.

In various corners we find holes scooped out. These are none other than the pits which yielded the clay for the statues. One of these basins still plainly shows the marks of the stone tools with which it was dug.

The mention of these basins brings me, in conclusion, to certain vestiges which abound here, 'vestiges so fragile and so strange,' writes Count Begouen, the prehistorian who has made the best study of the cavern, 'that we would hesitate to call them prehistoric if the whole fabric of circumstance did not assure us of the fact.' There are minute objects moulded in clay, and various unexpected signs of the complex Magdalenian psychology. I made a special study of the subject under the late Dr Capitan, who wrote: 'Strange though many of these manifestations may appear, their authenticity is beyond doubt. Many spots are covered with a thin stalagmitic deposit.'

The floor of the gallery and its walls, much smeared with clay, present an infinite variety of small modelled objects. The cracks of the rock have been carefully chinked, and then these bands of clay riddled with round holes; moulded balls the size of one's fist are deposited on ledges, sometimes in little heaps. Among these clay balls is one, differently shaped, which every one who has seen it believes is a slightly stylized female emblem. Clay plaster, stuck to the walls and sometimes to the ceiling, is full of holes punched with fingers or pointed sticks. One of these patches reproduces in cut-out outline the profile of a horse's head. This is the first such treatment ever found.

Equally unexpected are the pellets stuck to the rock. One of them, flattened like a wafer, holds against the wall a handsome flint chipped to the shape of a double scraper. The whole is now covered with a thin stalagmitic deposit. A kind of niche about sixteen inches high, fixed to the vertical wall, and showing marks of the fingers that made it, is also encased in stalagmite. In the same way a sort of swallow's nest of kneaded clay has been sealed to the wall.

Above the group of lions, in a rock crevice of several yards meticulously filled with kneaded clay and then punched full of holes, is stuck a large polished and curved bone spatula, a regular sculptor's boasting-tool which undoubtedly served in the making of the clay statues.

In the Hall of the Bear is a little font-shaped rock cavity, evidently a cache or a catch-all; rummaging, I found it full of chipped flints.

We find on the rock at the very end of the tunnel a series of radiating engraved lines, and heaped on the floor just below, a quantity of little pencil-like stalactites.

We can follow every step: the Magdalenians scooped up the clay by the handful, drew complicated networks and curlicues with their finger-tips, and planted or hid the flints. All these little operations, whose meaning still largely escapes us, have been obliterated in spots by the bears, which clawed the floor and walls. At Montespan, in fact, we notice many footprints of bears and of naked human feet.

Sometimes the claw-marks are on top of the footprints, sometimes the other way round; man and beast struggled for possession of the cavern. One can hardly think without shuddering of the fearful combats which must have taken place, nor ever cease to admire the courage of our distant ancestors who ventured into this lair of the wild beasts armed only with javelins and stone axes. The marvellous preservation of such curious remains is, of course, due to the fact that the cavern has been inaccessible from prehistoric times to the present day.

Of all the traces of a vanished age, the prints of hands and feet are perhaps the most impressive. I shall never forget my awe at first seeing these marks, intact after two hundred centuries of solitude. Such an experience repays in a moment all the hardships, risks, and countless disappointments which await those who would rob the jealous past of its secrets.

A study of the art at Montespan indicates that this is a sanctuary, one of those sacred grottoes where the sorcerers of hunting tribes in the reindeer age performed their magic ceremonies. The spells of modern diviners, still met with in civilized countries, seem thus but a lively remembrance of the cave-men.

In another chapter I shall discuss what is known of prehistoric magic. The many little bits of clay-work scattered through the cavern, such as sausage shapes, holes, networks, and honeycomb cells, are not yet understood. Some day, perhaps, these mysterious signs will be explained by comparison with analogous remains found in other caverns, along with new details which will give the key to the enigma.

2

THE SACRED GROTTO OF LABASTIDE

*

Ad augusta per angusta

*

IN April 1932, ten years after the discovery of the cavern of Montespan, I was on the borders of the Haute-Garonne and the Hautes-Pyrénées, at the extreme point of the fan-shaped plateau of Lannemezan, a vast wilderness of heath, gorse, and fern. From the top of this alluvial cone, built in geologic ages when the Pyrenees were far higher than now, one can see an unbroken and imposing 125-mile horizon. The giants of Aure and Bigorre stand out: the battlements of the Arbizon, the dome of the Pic du Midi, striped with snow, the Montaigu pyramid, and, far in the distance, the saw-toothed ridges of the frontier, the white Spanish peaks.

Among countless and nameless minor ridges in the foreground rises a wave of secondary peaks, forested with beech and fir. At the mouth of the Vallée d'Aure not far from the confluence of the Neste and the Garonne, is the grotto of Lortet, in a steep cliff washed by the Neste. This prehistoric dwelling-place was made famous by the excavations of Édouard Piette, starting in 1873. I passed it by, famous though it is, because the finds are now exhausted. Instead, I headed for an almost unknown and unexplored group of caverns between the Neste and Adour valleys, in the wooded, mountainous land of the Baronnies, which is, indeed, the 'land of the forty caverns'.

Going on information from my friend Léon Ducasse, Procureur of the Republic at Toulouse, who knows the region intimately, I began with the deep caverns of Labastide. They are near the village of the same name, which is strangely built in the bottom of a 250-acre funnel, encircled and dominated by the moors of Lannemezan and the foothills of the Pyrenees. In this basin there forms a brook which waters rich fields, goes through the village, and thence runs to the bottom of the hollow. Here its narrow, steep ravine ends at the mouth of a cavern called 'La Spugue,' where the water disappears through a narrow crevice. The underground watercourse comes to light again at the village of Esparros, a mile and a quarter away, penetrating the base of the intervening mountain from side to side. This 'hydrogeological penetration' is a common phenomenon in the chains of the Pyrenees.

The underground communication between Labastide and Esparros is obvious, but had been thought impossible to explore. The resurgence at Esparros is impassable, and the disappearance at Labastide appears too small for a man. In 1897 Armand Viré, the learned explorer of caverns, came to Labastide, but he, too, thought the stream impenetrable.

Being hardened to cold water and to the negotiation of difficult underground passages, I did not hesitate to pursue the watercourse on its way under ground. Undressing completely (clothes hold water, catch on projections, and are hampering and dangerous in caves), I slid head first into the descending fissure which swallows the brook.

It was the beginning of April – an unpropitious time, for the water was high and cold. I crawled desperately and with great difficulty between water and rock; then I moved flat on my stomach over a bed of soft and loathsome slime. My back was scraped by the low, rough ceiling. I was in constant fear for my light, which flickered in a strong air current. Finally, after great efforts, I got to the end of the flattened tunnel, where the gushing water had made a tremendous uproar. I was able to go on all fours, and soon, to stand upright in a beautiful hall, which I quickly crossed in my haste to get ahead.

I next entered a twisting gallery, but after going some 650 feet I was stopped by noxious gases, an insidious and indeed insuperable obstacle, which I soon discovered by the flickering of my lamp and by a strangling sensation.

I had time to make out in the darkness a great mass of leaves, grass, and various rubbish brought in from outside by a freshet. The rotting vegetable matter made it temporarily impossible to stay in that part of the cavern at all, and I had to beat a hasty retreat, deferring the exploration until another freshet should have carried the obstacle away. I returned to daylight without incident.

Without dressing I went to another cavern entrance which opened out of the same cliff in the same ravine as La Spugue. I got in by going down a steep slide of rubble into a sort of pit whose other walls are vertical. A hundred feet down is a beautiful archway, forming the dramatic entrance to this cave at the bottom of a well.

Daylight fades out most dangerously here. A few paces inward is another pit, wide and deep, occupying the whole breadth of the gallery. The only way around the pit is by a narrow ledge.

My acetylene lamp was working wretchedly that day; only my long practice underground enabled me to get about the huge cavern at all. The dark corridors were so vast that I decided to avoid getting lost by keeping to one wall all the time, and returning by the same route. Beyond the pit at the entrance, a rising gallery brought me to a hall; its level floor was cluttered with rocks, squat stalagmites, and animal bones brought in by foxes. I could also distinguish potsherds and a few human bones, remnants of habitation or of one of those miserable Neolithic and Gallic burial places which abound in the caves of the Pyrenees. Going on, I searched the cave for rock engravings, as I always do underground, but the rugged and scaly wall offered no place for prehistoric art. Of course, such discoveries are very rare, in any case.

I scaled several projections and a jumble of rocks, and crossed a long mire where I sank into sticky clay. Nine hundred and seventy-five feet (later measured) from daylight I reached a narrow hall ending in a cul-de-sac. The low ceiling and earth floor, apparently pounded and trampled, reminded me of the Hall of the Bear at Montespan. In several of the 300-odd caverns which I had then explored, I had had a similar feeling, a quite unfounded presentiment that I was about to find something startling. But this time my obstinacy was rewarded.

I raised my dim and smoky lamp. I had to half stoop and crane my neck to scrutinize the ceiling. I was startled and thrilled to find right over my head some of those scratched lines which never disappoint us who have hunted and deciphered prehistoric rock engravings. But I was too close to tell what the lines meant. Feverishly shaking my lamp, I profited by the increased light to lie on my back and study the markings on the ceiling.

Suddenly they took form as the astonishingly realistic head of a roaring lion. The head is larger than life. Its reality of expression is frightening: the muzzle is wrinkled, and the undershot jaw of the great open mouth gives the animal a ferocity accentuated by menacing canine teeth three inches long, and capped by the eye, squinting as the jaws stretch.

The man, the great artist, who scratched this masterpiece with a sharp pebble on the rugged ceiling, succeeded in reproducing faithfully, and with stunning intensity, a face-to-face encounter with the beast.

The reader can scarcely imagine my feelings. Alone in the bowels of the earth I was looking at art which made Egyptian antiquities seem young. I was the first, after how many centuries, to see the image of the terrible cave lion (*Felis leo* var. *spelaea*) which once haunted the forests and plains of what was to become my country.

Long years below ground in the Pyrenees had brought me this ultimate joy but twice – in 1923 at Montespan, and in 1930 in the grotto of Alquerdi (Spanish Navarre). There I had found drawings of bison and reindeer.

Some of the decorated caves of the Pyrenees have but two or three isolated designs. Labastide, I soon found, offered a whole prehistoric salon, a retrospective exhibition of incontestably the most interesting, the most moving, and the oldest art which exists. Magdalenian and its predecessor, Aurignacian, art date back, according to moderate estimates, 15,000 to 20,000 years before our era.

When at last I tore my eyes from the 'roaring lion,' I was sure I should see other drawings scratched in the rock. Sure enough, one of the chamber walls and part of the roof showed

Norbert Casteret

The Siphon at Montespan

Cave Scene

The Lance-pierced Lion

The Headless Bear

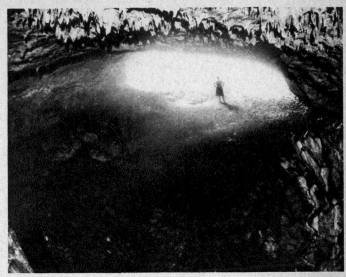

Mouth of the Grotto of Labastide

In the Hall of the Roaring Lion

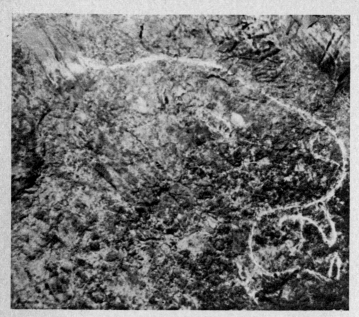

The Roaring Lion of Labastide

Engraving of a Prehistoric Horse

Labastide

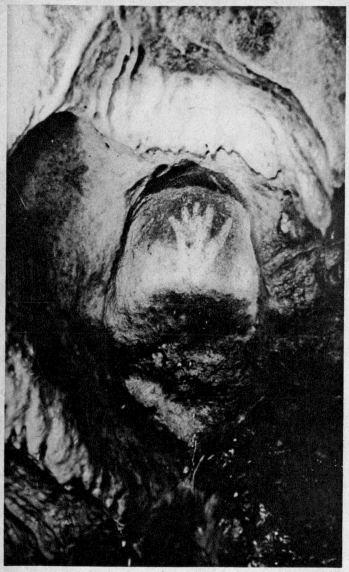

Imprint of a Mutilated Hand in the Grotto of Gargas

Stalactite Clubs and Daggers

8

an extraordinary tangle of designs. They were of all sizes, some deeply scratched with lines two fingers wide, others delicate, lightly traced, and visible only in strong light. The artist had sometimes superimposed as many as seven animals (a common prehistoric practice, where the designer worked over previous drawings, making an abstraction of them). But despite the frequent difficulty of deciphering these surcharges, I saw at a glance a long frieze of eight or ten horses, from five to six and a half feet long, following or facing one another. All these horses, and many others which I later found in other parts of the cave, had common characteristics – squat body, short, thick head, spiky, upright mane, and extremely long tail.

On the horse frieze are several bison and reindeer, a number of animals as yet unidentified, and a quantity of lines and symbols which defy explanation.

Particularly interesting is a distinct and detailed human head, something excessively rare in the records left by our infinitely distant ancestors. It is engraved in a depression in the wall, interrupting the horse frieze. Seen from the front it looks like a face framed in a loophole. The perfectly round face is most peculiar: the eyes are deeply incised circles; the nose is very large, and includes big, dilated nostrils, more animal than human; the mouth is a slash like that of a mask; a pointed beard completes this strange and bestial visage. There is a certain discomfort in reflecting that this may be a portrait. These men left great works behind to prove that they had risen farther than we think. Could they have looked like this? It is difficult to believe they resembled this figure in any way at all.

In my opinion – and I am not alone – this is a man in a sorcerer's mask, like those used by primitive peoples to-day. The snout and round eyes recall forcefully the celebrated masked sorcerer of the cavern of the Trois-Frères (Ariège) and the duk-duk masks of New Guinea.

Another engraving at Labastide represents a naked, masked man, his body stooped forward, his thighs bent, his arms held out horizontally before him. This is the posture of the 'Negro dance,' or rather, of a ritual dance which recurs in the similarly naked and masked sorcerer of the Trois-Frères, in the suppliants in the cavern of Altamira, and in the anthropomorphs (man-like creatures) of the caverns of the Combarelles and Marsoulas.

More naked and more solitary than the cave-dwellers (who never ventured underground alone), I was weighed down by the awful mystery of the accumulated centuries. But whatever my feelings, I had to think about my return; the hours had flown since I had entered the cavern, and the flame of my lamp sank ever lower. As I followed the wall almost blindly back to the entrance, I was already wondering when I could come again to finish exploring the cavern and to hunt for more engravings.

Outside I found the sun low in the sky. I was about to go down the steep slope to the mouth of the neighbouring cavern, where I had hidden my clothes, when I saw that the ravine was invaded by a flock of sheep and their taciturn shepherdess. Then I remembered that I was dressed for a swimming race, and covered with dirt and scratches. To avoid scandalizing the brown-skinned shepherdess I waited in the bushes until sunset took her and her white sheep toward the village.

Two days later I came back with my wife. In the course of fifteen sessions (the unexpected length of one of which brought the villagers to shout and wait for us in the evening at the cavern mouth) we found, copied, and photographed new drawings throughout the cave. We drew a plan by compass, but did not finish exploring, because there are pits leading to deep lower levels. We descended successive pits on a rope to a depth of 195 feet, and were stopped by lack of rope at a last yawning chasm which went yet deeper into the bowels of the mountain.

The top level was the only one frequented by man. On isolated blocks, on walls and roof we found engravings of horses, reindeer, bison, bears, felines, wild goats, boars, and a goose. The predominance of horse drawings, however, caused me to christen this the *Grotte des Chevaux*, to distinguish it from several neighbouring caverns all lumped together as the grottoes of Labastide.

Some of the designs are Aurignacian. They are more defaced and less skilful, because much older, than those of the Magdalenian period – the age rightly called the epoch of the prehistoric Fine Arts.

Six hundred and fifty feet from the entrance, an enormous rock, fallen from the high ceiling, partially blocks the main gallery. On the flat surface of this rock is a horse, engraved in line and painted in red. The mane and hoofs alone are black. The animal is extremely large, and its head is nearly ten feet from the ground. This is the only specimen of painting in the cavern (prehistoric paintings are, incidentally, even rarer than engravings).

At the end of the cavern, on an earthy path more than 1,300 feet in, are two large circles made of stones touching one another in the manner of cromlechs. Within the circles are charcoal, charred bones, horses' jaws and teeth, and chipped flints. There are also reindeer-horn javelin-points, and several limestone slabs with fine engravings of horses, reindeer, bison, mammoths, and a bear's head. All these slabs were lying on the ground face down. This is undoubtedly part of some rite, for the same thing has been noticed in other caverns.

There is much to say about the remains and engravings in the cavern, and about some characteristic peculiarities. Once more we are faced with the problem of the meaning of the designs. Why were they executed in the remotest spots, in difficult and, sometimes, quite improbable positions?

Thanks to such men as Cartailhac, Capitan, Breuil, and Begouen, the theory of prehistoric magic has prevailed over the essentially literary theory of 'art for art's sake'. We are no longer surprised to find the works of art in inaccessible parts of a few rare grottoes, and the explanation is now plain for the puzzling silhouettes of masked men, sometimes completely disguised, who preside over scenes of sorcery and witchcraft in several of the caverns. The sorcerer is perfectly in place amid such a witches' sabbath.

3

DIGGING

*

Lifeless objects, yet you have a soul
LAMARTINE

*

IT is an August noon in a lonely valley of Comminges, pic-turesquely situated in the foothills of the Central Pyrenees – marvellous Comminges, so fertile in traces of the past. After a long, hot bicycle trip I go down a rocky road, steep as a toboggan slide, which ends at a brook-bed in a mire where the Gascon cows sink to the hocks when they come to drink. Leaving my wheel in a jungle of horsetails and ferns where it will be shaded and out of sight, I head for a cave.

The way leads up the brook-bed through some woods, across fields, along the side of a parched hillock. There are swarms of grey grasshoppers, and the piercing hum of the cicadas is everywhere. Above the ravine a cave-mouth yawns among the junipers, their scent heightened by the heat.

Here I have been digging patiently for a year in a little grotto which has yielded the rich store of an Aurignacian hearth. I breathe the cave's cool scent of moss, earth, and rock. As my eyes grow used to the gloom I recognize the round chamber and the familiar details – the heap of rubbish, which grows at each visit, the flat slab which serves as seat and some-times as dining-table, the one column where I hang my bag on a projection.

A glance is enough to tell me that nothing has changed since my last visit. Taking out the acetylene lamp and a linen overall stained with the clay of many a cavern, I hang the bag up on the pillar. I put on the overall, and go to a tiny basin to dip water for the lantern. The hissing lantern is soon giving a fine, lurid light; the grotto, completely illuminated, becomes more intimate.

The cave-men who dwelt here made a good choice: it was dry, healthy, and without draught; its mouth, with a southern exposure, could be closed with a few branches or a skin. What went on in this grotto? How many centuries was it inhabited? How many thousands of years since it was first used? For months I have been piously removing the ashes of our ancestors, trying to answer the question of the past.

From a crack in the rock I take out a short pick, a steel hook, a hammer, and a cold chisel. Kneeling, with lamp and tools on the ground beside me, I examine the state of the work. I have undertaken to dig up the grotto in nine-inch slices.

Layer by layer I have reached a depth of three feet, recording daily the location of the various finds and the nature of the substances encountered – stalagmite, clay, broken stone, earth.

The floor of the cavern before being attacked is a thick, hard layer of stalagmite. This floor I break up and remove in slabs. The compact clay beneath has surrendered various scattered relics – flint tools and weapons, engraved bones, many animal bones brought in by man. Among the latter was a rhinoceros skull, the pride of my collection.

To-day I work in the midst of an Aurignacian hearth. My hook, cautiously wielded, exposes bit by bit a heterogeneous mass – hardened ashes, charcoal, broken bones, flint chips, pebbles. The various elements of the pot-pourri are separated, examined, sorted, and shoved back to the rubbish heap. I attack a new part. By working in this way I am sure of virgin layers, which I have gradually learned to read like a book.

This sort of prospecting soon takes one captive – no need of finding museum pieces to become fascinated with the game. One is in direct communication with prehistoric ages, living in a sort of intimacy with primitive man.

The freshly cut earth is full of wood charcoal and bone splinters. A bluish flint point comes to light. Will it be a trifling fragment, a broken blade? The steel finger of the hook probes the clay all around, feeling for the length of the object.

It is deeply imbedded, and therefore fairly large. I must work with caution.

As it enlarges the hole, the hook grates on another hard, shiny body. The ivory of a tooth appears; now it is free. Heavy and shining, with characteristic rectangular shape and groovings, this strong horse molar seems as if it had been buried yesterday. But so do all the bones. Protected from the air, they slowly continue to fossilize in the compact clay.

The flint, my real object, is jammed between two stones, and resists the timid urging of my fingers. I have to dig further, crush pieces of charcoal, disentangle a jumble of gravel and bones. Finally, the flint stirs in the gangue, its slenderness allows me to pull it from its resting-place. Here it is, bare in my hand, just as on the day it was fashioned with such patience and such skill. It is bluish, and translucent, and cool. The facets from the blows with which it was shaped are skilfully distributed, and it sits well in the hand.

A violent blow of the pick at the front of the cutting knocks off a chunk, on which I concentrate intently. The sorting and inventory of this mass of earth are a long task. Infiltrations of water, charged with dissolved limestone, have formed stalagmite, which seals the object in a natural cement, called *breccia*. I clean off one after another a reindeer horn with distinct marks of a flint saw; a wolf's canine tooth pierced for a necklace; finally, a rib from some large animal, its flat surface covered with almost invisible tracery.

At a bound I am in daylight at the entrance. Spitting on my finger I rub off the sticky yellow clay which covers the bone. The fine engraving sees again the light that shone on it aeons ago. It is a trout with outspread fins; on its back is an arrow, the prophetic harpoon – the traditional magic spell.

The rib is wrapped in my handkerchief with infinite care, and put in the bag; it will be washed and minutely studied later. For the present the digging goes forward.

In the cool of the cavern I can forget the uncomfortable posture and tiring work; pick and hook are not idle, hammer and chisel finish the work in the hard, bone-bearing breccia. The edge of the digging moves back, the rubbish piles up, and the little store of treasures grows – chipped flints, pierced teeth and shells, bone javelin-heads and needles. The hours pass. . . .

The patch of sky in the cave mouth darkens; it is time to think of going back. The tools are hidden again; the bag is fat and heavy on my hip; I say au revoir to this home of ancestral memories. I have to wrench myself from the past. Two bats, disturbed by me, or drawn by the night, pass the threshold of the cave as I do, skimming me in their noiseless flight.

It is dusk of a calm, beautiful day. The brook winds through woods and meadows at the bottom of the lonely ravine. It murmurs as it murmured aeons ago when the men came back from the hunt; women and children hurried for the cave and safety, their arms filled with a harvest of snails, berries, and roots. At nightfall then, this ravine swarmed with life: bison and horse gathered on the fringes of the woods, the bear slunk from his lair to go marauding, and the lions, the wolves, the hyenas began the hunt with a wild and frightful concert. It was a savage age of fear, of struggle for life. In such surroundings, after a day of solitary communion with the past, it rises, as if present, before us.

The yap of a fox leaving for the chase in the inky woods under the first stars of evening completes the illusion; it rouses a vague, atavistic longing for ages dead and gone.

Fumbling, I recover my bicycle from the bushes. The mere touch of the handle-bars breaks the spell; I am nothing now but a cyclist belated on a bad road. Carrying the wheel, I am fording the brook on stones when a splash, followed by something plunking into the water, makes me jump. A trout has just leaped. I smile: at the bottom of my bag is the fine engraved trout from the prehistoric hearth. I shall admire it under the lens this evening, thinking of the Aurignacian enchanter who drew his spells on bone before he dangled his bait in the brook – at the same time of the evening as now, perhaps at the very spot where the fish just leaped.

PART TWO

PREHISTORIC MAGIC

*

The primitive magic which we know is inextricably entangled
with religion
JOSEPH MAXWELL, *La Magie*

I

MAGIC IN PREHISTORIC TIMES

*

The coercive action of man upon nature is the
origin of magic
JOSEPH MAXWELL, *La Magie*

*

THE study of prehistoric archaeology scarcely goes back
further than 1840. Until then, those who tried to pursue man
through the centuries were halted for lack of written documents beyond the Egyptian and Chinese civilizations, a few
centuries before Christ.

It was left for French scholars to discover on their native
soil traces of human industry which set back the date of man's
appearance to an apparently fabulous antiquity. These discoveries made man a contemporary of the mammoth and of
other 'antediluvian' animals; they were so unexpected that the
scientific world refused to accept them.

The illustrious Boucher de Perthes, the founder of prehistory, had to fight for years before his work was accepted
and given the accolade of the Institut. There was violent
polemic activity, but Boucher de Perthes excavated for seventeen years in the valley of the Somme, and his final results made

doubt impossible. Science admitted the extreme antiquity of man.

From then on, people dug up cave bottoms and valley soil; discoveries multiplied, and slowly, patiently, the chronology of the Stone Age was established. Prehistoric archaeology has since revealed much about the life and customs of the first men.

One of the most astonishing discoveries is that primitive man knew, and practised, magic.

The subject of prehistoric magic is so unexpected as to require some explanation. Without previous study it is hard to imagine, much less admit, that our ancestors of perhaps 25,000 years ago performed occult ceremonies. But we find that the practice of witchcraft and magic is common even to-day in direct proportion to the backwardness of the population; among savage tribes, which are still in the Stone Age, and thus comparable to the hordes of prehistory, magic is highly honoured. The witch-doctor is the most powerful and most feared personage of the tribe.

It is probably in the Aurignacian epoch (named from the celebrated grotto of Aurignac in the Haute-Garonne) that we find the first real art – designs scratched on bone and pebbles and cave walls. One of the first prehistoric designs found was in the grotto of Massat (Ariège). It represents a bear. People doubted its authenticity for a while, but similar finds multiplied everywhere. The evidence was compelling: primitive man practised design. He represented all the animals around him, sometimes naïvely, sometimes with gripping realism.

No one now doubts that for many centuries man used arms and tools of stone, which he chipped out with great pains. They are found by the thousand on the floors of the caves he inhabited. Nor does any one contest that man has left engravings and paintings on the walls of these same caverns. But for some years people have been asking what these designs mean.

There are two theories. Some persons maintain that the cave man drew for pastime, for the mere pleasure of drawing. This 'art-for-art's-sake' theory loses adherents every day, and

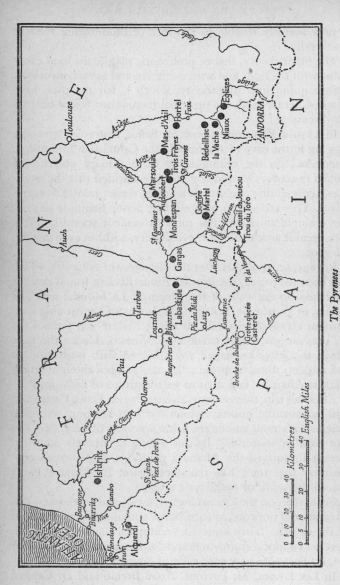

The Pyrenees

The fourteen painted caverns are marked thus ●. For map of the Trou du Toro and Gouell region see p. 182.

is now scarcely tenable in the face of illuminating modern discoveries.

The other theory, that of prehistoric magic, fits in at every point with the finds and with primitive and savage mentality. Before going into this theory, which I, for my part, have adopted, let us recall the principal discoveries which bear on the discussion.

In 1879 a Barcelona advocate, Señor Santuola, who was digging in the cave of Altamira in the Cantabrian Mountains, discovered on the ceiling some extraordinary polychrome animal frescoes. On studying them he decided that the paintings, representing prehistoric animals, were prehistoric themselves. This seemed so unlikely that Señor Santuola did not win a single adherent. The most prominent scientists wrote disagreeable articles about the discovery, without even visiting the spot.

In 1895, sixteen years after the discovery of Altamira, which had been forgotten, the learned Émile Rivière found designs scratched on the walls of the cavern of La Mouthe near Les Eyzies, in Dordogne. Señor Santuola was an almost unknown amateur archaeologist, but M. Émile Rivière was famous for his excavations in the caverns of Monaco. Hence the note which the latter published was received with more caution and respect; the savants did what they had not thought worth while at Altamira, and went to see the grotto of La Mouthe.

After this trip, the celebrated archaeologist, Émile Cartailhac, with a scientific honesty which did him honour, wrote an article still famous among the bitter wrangles of the time: 'The *mea culpa* of a sceptic.' In this article he bravely admitted having misjudged the Altamira paintings, and proved conclusively that they, like the drawings at La Mouthe, were indeed the work of prehistoric artists.

From then on the archaeologists, awakened by the new discoveries, did not content themselves with digging up the floor of the caverns. They minutely scrutinized the walls, and discoveries of mural engravings and paintings multiplied as if by magic. There are sixty such caverns now known.

In Les Eyzies, M. Peyroni, Abbé Breuil, and Dr Capitan

uncovered the masterpieces of the Combarelles, of Font-de-Gaume, and others. In the Pyrenees, at the grotto of Marsoulas, frescoes and engravings were discovered. At Gargas are many drawings and curious hand-prints.

In the immense cavern of Niaux, Commandant Molard discovered, in 1906, the most beautiful prehistoric designs known. Still in the Pyrenees, we find works of art in the caves of the Mas d'Azil, of the Portel, of the Trois-Frères, of Isturitz, and others.

In 1913 came a new sensational discovery: Count Begouen and his three sons found the statuettes of bison modelled in clay in the depths of the Tuc d'Audoubert grotto. The announcement of this discovery, like all others dealing with prehistory, was received with a stir of incredulity. We must remember, however, that this find was truly extraordinary. How could statuettes of raw clay have been preserved in such perfect condition? They were still plastic; not the least deposit, no sign of age spoke for their vast antiquity.

But no one who has seen the bisons at the bottom of the cavern (where they still are), and who has seen the wall drawings and the footprints of bears and prehistoric men, can still have doubts. Prehistorians have flocked to the cavern.

In 1922 Abbé Lemozy discovered at Cabrerets, in the Lot, a vast cavern filled with engravings and paintings. In 1923 I found the engravings and prehistoric clay statues in the cavern of Montespan. This was of great importance because the clay bisons of the Tuc d'Audoubert had remained unique for ten years, and their state of preservation still called forth implications unkind and unjust to the Begouens, discoverers of one of the purest masterpieces of Magdalenian art.

The Montespan discovery banished all doubts, because some of the statues are covered with limestone deposits which form extremely slowly.

Materials for study are now abundant, and they multiply every day. The theory of prehistoric magic which seemed far-fetched a few years ago is now accepted by the most eminent scholars.

The decorated caverns are all either well hidden or difficult and dangerous of access. Furthermore, the figures used for the ceremonies are at a distance (sometimes a long distance) from daylight, and by preference in the best-hidden recesses. In fact, prehistoric sorcerers usually established their sanctuaries in narrow, twisting tunnels, far from profane eyes.

At Marsoulas, the excavations of Abbé Cau-Durban allowed the clearing out of the gallery where the engravings are. Originally, one could get in only by crawling on all fours.

At Pasiega, in Spain, the medicine-men entered the cavern by a narrow, steep pit. The cavern of Pindal, also in Spain,

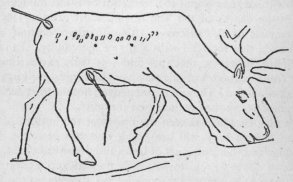

Grazing reindeer engraved on stone 25,000 years ago at the settlement of Limeuil, Dordogne

opens on the sea from an abrupt cliff. The deep gallery, painted with reindeer, bison, and rhinoceros, in the cavern of Font-de-Gaume can be reached only by squeezing through a rat-hole called the Passage of the Rubicon.

At the Combarelles is a long, narrow corridor which forces one to stoop or walk on one's knees; the engravings cannot be seen until half-way down the cavern. At La Mouthe a tube had to be cleared out before the designs were discovered on the ceilings, where they could be reached only by crawling. In the cavern of Niaux, the hall of the drawings is half a mile from the entrance. The cavern of the Trois-Frères is an endless succession of corridors and chambers; the decorated walls are half an hour's walk underground.

At the Tuc d'Audoubert, visitors canoe up the underground course of the Volp, climb to a higher level by pegs and iron ladders, and wriggle through low-ceilinged corridors before reaching the last hall, where the two celebrated clay bisons and many wall engravings are. The cavern of Cabrerets is a veritable labyrinth; the remains which abound there were found by several hours' crawling.

It would be easy, but useless, to list all the decorated grottoes, and to point out how well their difficulty of access suits them to ceremonies requiring solitude and mystery.

The Aurignacians and the Magdalenians, hunters at heart, tried to make their hunting successful by ceremonies whose meaning grows clearer and clearer as prehistoric discoveries multiply. They would draw the animals they wanted to kill; then, as a magic spell, they would mark wounds on the drawings. They killed the animal in effigy, as it were, to make sure of killing the actual creature which they had thus bewitched.

This explains the signs, the holes, the arrows, axes, and clubs which are found on many of the animal drawings. Sometimes the intention of the primitive huntsman is even more explicit: the animal is shown in a trap, a snare, or being stoned. The theory is proved almost beyond doubt by the lions and bear of Montespan, which are riddled with the marks of javelins and arrows, thrown so violently at the vital spots that some of the statues have collapsed.

This interpretation of the mutilations is further strengthened by the cub's skull at the feet of the headless bear. To give the spell more effect, and to make the bear's double as like as possible, the Magdalenian wizards, as we have seen, fastened to the clay statue the head of a bear recently killed. Upon this, the ancestor of all witches' poppets, they practised their incantations and their sham combat, accompanied by dances and ritual chants which we shall never know.

It is interesting to observe that at Montespan only savage beasts are mutilated. This does not break down the theory of magic; it confirms it.

The Magdalenians, who believed they had occult power over the lives of the animals they feared, believed they could also increase the fertility of the species on which they lived.

Spells of this sort must have been at least as common as the other kind, for the periods of intense cold caused great migrations of bison, horse, and reindeer, and thus long and terrible famines.

Some of the prehistoric relics are incontestably peaceful witchcraft, unequivocal symbols of fecundity. Thus several of the Montespan animals have large and pendulous bellies. This deliberate exaggeration seems intended to represent females with young. It is reasonable to think that the witch-doctor who drew the animals was assisting by enchantment in the reproduction of certain species which prehistoric man consumed in enormous quantity, as shown by the heaps of bones so often found.

One of the gravid mares of Montespan has engraved on her shoulder a right hand, true symbol of man's domination over the animal. Another mare, modelled in clay, shows in exaggerated fashion a detail scarcely visible in reality – swollen nipples, which can hardly be explained except by the intention I have just suggested.

As for the bison pair of Tuc d'Audoubert, I know no better way of describing them than by quoting the passage concerning them in the prehistoric novel based on scientific fact, *Les Bisons d'argile*, by Max Begouen.

The sorcerer, or shaman, starts to execute the famous sculptures:

All the anatomical details emerged minutely under the fingers of the magician. Soon the men could see a female bison with neck outstretched, seeming to bellow and sniff the cold air of the steppe. Next the shaman modelled the male bison in the same fashion; he made it stronger than the female, with cruder forms, just as in reality. And his modelling was coarser, less detailed. . . . The rock being too small, the sorcerer had to prop up the statue of the male bison with a stone and a chunk of clay, and thus he gave the group the posture necessary for fecundity – a female bison, followed by a bull half upright on his hind legs.

Spells, destructive and protective, were the great preoccupations, the touchstone of hunters' magic, in prehistoric times. For that matter, what of to-day? Not a primitive tribe of the present but is familiar with the magic of the hunt, and follows ceremonies and practices inherited directly from the cave men.

In the famous American Indian buffalo dance, the hunters, covered with buffalo robes, executed ritual dances and sham combats; this was nothing but an incantation, a spell to aid the hunt and to keep the herds from leaving the hunting grounds.

The day before scal-hunts and fishing expeditions the Eskimos have analogous ceremonies and pantomimes. Before hunting the emu the Australian natives draw the image of the bird on the ground, and riddle it with arrows and execrations.

Who can still doubt that magic is universal, and prehistoric in origin?

2

PUZZLES AND CURIOSITIES OF PREHISTORIC ART

*

I want to show all we owe to those remote ages,
all that those ages have left with us
FUSTEL DE COULANGES

*

By now such a mass of prehistoric art has been discovered that no one book reproduces it all.

Prehistoric artists confined themselves almost entirely to animals; we have seen that some of their works in this field are absolute masterpieces. With rare exceptions the vegetable kingdom did not interest them, but geometric designs (apparently inspired by nothing in nature) were in considerable favour.

The stone-age artist's equipment was elementary. To engrave his designs on bone, ivory, pebbles, even on the rugged rock of the caverns, he had nothing but patiently chipped flint gravers. The point, soon blunted, needed to be sharpened by fresh chipping all the time.

For painting, man has no doubt always used the juice of berries, but these perishable colours have not survived. On the other hand, two very common natural oxides, iron oxide and manganese peroxide, yield colours which defy time and moisture. Iron oxide suitably pounded up and mixed with water or animal fat produced a range of colours from ochre to red and vermilion (for which prehistoric man seemed to have a special fondness); manganese peroxide yielded browns and black. With this scanty palette all the prehistoric paintings were made; yet the great polychrome fresco of Altamira is forty-five feet long, with twenty-five almost life-sized animals.

For carving wood, bone, and stone no tools were available

beyond flint gravers, scrapers, and drills. Flint was the only mineral whose hardness and flaky structure made possible the manufacture of weapons and tools for early man. Alike for the carving of such bas-reliefs as that of Cap-Blanc (Dordogne), with its life-sized horses, and for making bone needles with tiny eyes, our ancestors knew no tool but flint.

Modern artists would hardly trade their pencils and brushes for a sharpened pebble or a finger dipped in paint; still less paint on rugged stone, where the preliminary scrawls of the sketch can never be erased. Yet the prehistoric masterpieces were all made in that way.

What sort of men were these, then? They were tens of centuries away from the use of metals, of pottery, of building, and they had every appearance of barbarism; yet their intelligence was no less remarkable than their feeling for art. Here we touch on one of the most obscure and fascinating questions of prehistory. Prehistoric man was primitive, but not savage. The savages of the present are not retarded primitives, but backsliders who have moved in the opposite direction from the rest of humanity.

There can be no doubt that intellectually prehistoric man was many centuries ahead of his material status. If he had not been, he probably would never have emerged from his miserable condition. We, his heirs, therefore, must study primitive man with pride and gratitude. We are the descendants of those who did battle against ages of savagery for the title of lords of creation.

The very first prehistoric art appears at the end of the Mousterian epoch; it multiplies and improves during the Aurignacian, and reaches its height with the Magdalenians.

It is futile to translate prehistoric chronology into figures; but estimates by the most distinguished and cautious scientists place the Mousterian epoch about 50,000 years, the Aurignacian 25,000, and the Magdalenian between 15,000 and 20,000 years before Christ. Thus each of them lasted considerably longer than our own brief historical epoch.

The art relics of the Mousterian period (grotto of the Moustier, Dordogne) consist of a few slabs of rough rock, in which we can distinguish cupules, incisions, and vague animal-like shapes. These natural slabs were discovered in caves abounding in Mousterian relics – chipped flints, broken and charred animal bones, hearths.

The ornaments are simple scrawls and outlines, so clumsy that one hesitates to speak of Mousterian *art*. But it is nevertheless true that the first rudiments of decoration, and hence of art, date from this period. Here was the dawn of that feeling for design which had such free rein in the succeeding epochs.

The Mousterians were a low order of man, with an ugly, bestial silhouette like the Neanderthal man. After them came the Aurignacians, of the Cro-Magnon race, harmonious in proportions and tall of stature. These men were the first to leave behind countless childish drawings of the animals of their age – mammoth, bison, stag, reindeer, horse, bear, wild goat, etc.

All the animals are recognizable, but they share certain defects of execution and technique. The silhouette is stiff and often clumsy; the head, no matter of what animal, has an annoying tendency to a pointed muzzle; the feet are ill-handled or missing.

Not until the Solutrean, and above all the Magdalenian era, do we find the designs correct and true to nature. Such designs as the grazing reindeer of Thayngen (Switzerland) and that of Limeuil (Dordogne) are masterpieces of exact observation. Further, the mastery of the artists is proved by the truly astonishing fact that the Magdalenians used daring techniques – imaginative and unconventional concepts which reappeared only in the twentieth century as modernist and futurist schools.

Stylization to-day is used to startle and to shock; stylization rules art, illustration, advertising. Objects and people are represented by symbols and lines deliberately distorted. Some of those who believe they are innovators will be surprised to learn that the cave men stylized their drawings – not, it is true, out of snobbery or affectation, but with some occult purpose.

Among these primitive conventions are symbols called pectiform (comb-shaped), tectiform (roof-shaped), and claviform (axe-shaped); they represent in simplified form the hand, the hut, and the hatchet. These symbols, a sort of *leitmotiv* in palaeolithic art, are sometimes accompanied by the symbol of water, so that all the material interests necessary to existence are there reflected.

We have already seen that the stylized hand (the pectiform of the archaeologists) appears on many animal drawings. It is usually on the beast's flank, symbolizing the hunter's domination over the animal.

The tectiform, a hut drawn with a few lines, shows that our ancestors could house themselves in structures of branches when no cave was handy. The claviform stands for the stone axe and the club, and occurs both alone and near animals.

It would be worth while to devote a chapter to the long series of stylized emblems concerned with the secret of generation. The various signs thus far described were unquestionably used for magical or religious purposes, but there are also true stylizations of purely decorative effect, bizarre whims of the artist. Among these are curious full-face horse heads on bone rods.

Sometimes the artist did not deform his work according to ritual, but instead, urged by a fertile imagination and a skilful hand, used a style which has since rallied a whole school – pointillism. The most characteristic prehistoric painting of this type is in the grotto of Marsoulas (Haute-Garonne): a great bison, made entirely of juxtaposed fat red daubs. The effect is stunning.

Even cubism boasts a prehistoric ancestry. There are a few attempts, rare indeed, but just enough to show that the Magdalenians tried it out, and had the taste to go back at once to sane and natural representations of the animals of their time. The best sample of unconventionality is the famous walking boar of the Altamira cavern, which has no less than eight legs. The slow-motion analysis of walking is more curious than correct, and the whole impression is grotesque.

After the Magdalenian epoch there are among prehistoric remains hardly any traces of animal art, and very few of decorative art. This may have something to do with the fact that man thereafter, absorbed in his first efforts to domesticate animals and practise cultivation, had neither the leisure nor the magical beliefs of the Magdalenian hunters.

Prehistoric art, thus highly developed, yet without successors, still fascinates us across the ages. Many of its secrets still remain to tantalize us.

3

THE ODDITY OF HUMAN FIGURES IN PRIMITIVE ART

*

Cursed be the man that maketh any graven image
DEUTERONOMY xxvii. 15

*

CONSIDERING the profusion with which our ancestors decorated the caverns, the rarity of human figures is striking. Not only are they rare, but people have long wondered why prehistoric men, who reproduced animals in every attitude so skilfully, have left us only strange and grotesque caricatures of their own kind. Such difference cannot be due to the awkwardness of the artist; there must be some other reason.

In their efforts to explain the anomaly, prehistorians have resorted, as in many other questions, to comparative ethnography. A knowledge of the customs and beliefs of modern savages has in fact provided the solution of many a prehistoric puzzle.

Every one knows the dislike of many primitive peoples and some civilized ones for being photographed. A number of explorers have been killed or outraged for ignoring this objection. In other cases the artist or photographer may see the natives fleeing as fast as their legs will carry them, or obstinately hiding their faces.

According to circumstances the reaction is angry or timid, but the fear has a reason. The white man with his innumerable inventions is an alarming being anyway; but what the savage fears above everything is to have a stranger get possession of his picture.

By getting your portrait I acquire your double, in the magical sense of the word, and I am then able to bewitch you, and work all sorts of mischief upon you. Prehistoric men, who after all were the creators of magic, knew this perfectly well; and so they carefully avoided reproducing the human figure except under special circumstances, and then with elaborate precautions.

Palaeolithic depictions of man fall into three types, all equally curious, and all characterized by evident intent never to show the face without deforming it.

First come clearly and unmistakably human figures which, realistic though they be, have no face, or at best a very imperfect one. Second we have faces where the features are accentuated, exaggerated, and often strangely interpreted. These, it seems, are men in masks. This explains the curious human profiles in certain caverns, characterized by enormous eyes, a nose like a beak or a muzzle, and huge ears. Finally there is a third category: grotesque beings of which it was long uncertain whether they were men or animals. They are men masked and completely disguised.

To the first category belong a series of figurines found near Aurignacian hearths from the Pyrenees to Russia. The statuettes are closely related by technique and by certain peculiarities of form, and they clearly mark the limits of distribution of the Aurignacians.

The point of similarity which is remarkable to us is that all the artists who carved the statuettes deliberately omitted the face. The 'Venus' of Willendorf (Austria) and that of Lespugue (Haute-Garonne) are astonishingly realistic and carefully shaped in every other way, but they have no faces. The front of the head, quite without features, is almost entirely covered with dangling hair.

One lonely statuette of the period is an exception to the rule: a little ivory head of a woman from the Grotte du Pape at Brassempouy (Landes). This head, known under the name of the Figurine with the Hood, represents a woman whose braided hair is gathered in a net. The face is suggested, nose and nostrils being shown, but no further details finish it, and it remains perforce without character or expression.

At Laussel (Dordogne) Dr Lalanne discovered some bas-reliefs, the best preserved of which represents a naked woman holding a bison horn in her hand. The sculpture is modelled with the greatest care, but true to the Aurignacian rule there is no face.

In short, all the thirty known Aurignacian statues are without face. There is no complete agreement about the meaning of this singular absence, but of the fact there can be no doubt.

On the other hand there are, as I have said, human figures with features so strange and exaggerated that there is reason

Prehistoric wall engravings of masks from the Grotte de Marsoula

to believe they are masked. The famous drawings in the caverns of Marsoulas and the Combarelles alone would suffice to show that these round eyes and enormous crooked noses could belong only to masks.

The mask among primitive peoples is seldom a plaything; it is used for ritual, war, or the chase. It is indispensable to the Negro witch-doctor; with its help he assumes a frightful appearance, which spreads dismay among the audience at his magic ceremonies and incantations.

The most interesting picture of a prehistoric magician is

that discovered by Count Begouen and his three sons in the cave of the Trois-Frères, near Saint-Girons (Ariège).

The wizard, whose body is painted with ritual red and black, is shown dancing naked, but, as Count Begouen describes him, 'He has gloved his hands in the skin of a lion's paws, with sharp claws; he is hidden behind a mask with the beard of a bison, an eagle's beak, the eyes of an owl, a wolf's ears, and a stag's antlers. He has fastened a horse-tail to the base of his spine. Thus he believes he has taken on all the magic power, all the physical qualities of the animals: the bravery of the lion, the sharp sight of the eagle by day and of the owl by night, the hearing of the wolf, the endurance of the bison, the speed of horse and stag.'

This sorcerer is engraved and painted ten feet above the floor at the end of a hall 1,625 feet from daylight. He has the place of honour in a natural amphitheatre; ranged at his feet is a long procession of animals engraved on the rock: lions, tigers, reindeer, bison, bears, dziggetai, which are marked with wounds, arrows, clubs, in a word with all the paraphernalia of hunter's witchcraft. On the clay floor one may still see (now religiously preserved) the bare footprints of the men who once went through their ceremonies here.

In the light of these relics we can reasonably imagine the arrival of the sorcerer. By the pale light of a stone lamp, its moss wick dipped in animal fat, he would come to the sanctuary in his frightful disguise, and perform the mysterious rites of his religion.

He attempts with his incantations and his spells scratched on the rock to draw to his tribe the good will of occult forces. He prays after his fashion that his people may be protected from tigers, from lions and bears, that they may never lack the meat of bison, horse, and reindeer, that their warriors may triumph in combat and in the chase.

Such masked and partially disguised figures as the Sorcerer of the Trois-Frères cavern bring us to the third category of human figures – those masked and completely disguised.

These bizarre creatures, animal in form, but human in attitude, were identified by MM. Cartailhac, Capitan, and

Breuil, the three scholars who discovered the existence of magic in primitive ages. According to prehistorians, the figures wear hunting or war disguises.

Comparative ethnography has performed a great service in explaining this most curious and puzzling aspect of prehistory.

THE PHANTOM HANDS OF GARGAS

*

Let us collect facts in order to have ideas
BUFFON

*

IN a certain few decorated caverns there exist, in addition to paintings and drawings, some curious coloured hand-prints. The cavern of Gargas contains about 200, most of them mutilated. They can be explained only by the ever-faithful help of comparative ethnography.

Voluntary mutilation, the amputation of phalanges or of entire fingers, is still practised by some savage peoples. The meaning and extent of these blood sacrifices vary according to locality; but the mutilation shows a stoicism and a touching devotion among people often wrongly thought lacking in sentiment. Usually the mutilations commemorate an unhappy occurrence; in fact we can almost say that originally they were always a sign of mourning.

The Bushmen of Central Africa cut off a phalange from the third or the little finger (using a flint knife) as a sign of grief when a member of the family dies. The Hottentots cut off the little finger to drive away illness. Some of the Canadian Indians cut off the third finger if there have been a number of deaths in the same family, as a means of warding off further visitations. In the Fiji Islands, at the death of a chief a hundred fingers had to be cut off. These are but a few random samples of a practice which exists throughout the world.

People who have thus mutilated themselves have apparently always tried to perpetuate the memory of their sacrifice. To this attempt we owe some surprising finds which show that the custom of mutilation and of hand-prints is prehistoric.

Once again the caverns of France have furnished us with

fascinating discoveries. The Pyrenean grottoes of Gargas, Bédeilhac, the Trois-Frères, of Cabrerets (Lot), and of Altamira and Castillo in Spain, among others, contain hand-prints, but the cavern of Gargas is the most interesting. This cave, near Luchon and Saint-Bertrand-de-Comminges, contains fine chambers which were inhabited by cave men, chiefly the Aurignacians. Great hearths have furnished a precious harvest of chipped flints, bone and ivory articles, and great quantities of bones from animals used as food.

The Aurignacians decorated the walls of the cavern with clumsy primitive drawings, among which we recognize bison,

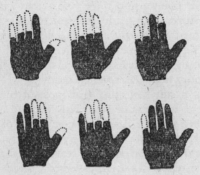

The mutilations most frequent among the Gargas hand-prints

horses, and wild goats. But the collection of fearfully mutilated hand-prints in every corner of the cavern gives the frescoes their chief interest. We cannot study this testimony of our ancestors' sorrow without being deeply moved. The cult of the dead is the oldest known to humanity.

The hand-prints were of two kinds, positive and negative. The positive technique is the simpler, but the more rarely used. It consisted in smearing the inside of the hand with paint (powdered ochre or manganese mixed with animal fat), and pressing the hand against the rock. The imprint appeared in red or black on the wall of the cavern.

The making of negative imprints was probably a more elaborate and mysterious rite. The man would press his hand to the rock, and daub all around it with paint. This, of course, left a 'phantom hand' of a lighter colour on a red or black ground. Some of the negative hands are so clear-cut that it seems the operator must have sprayed on liquid paint with his mouth.

The hands of Gargas show the entire scale of mutilations from a single phalange to complete absence of fingers, the hand remaining but a stump. In general, the mutilations are more drastic than those practised in modern times.

One more fact calls for mention: there were many children among the victims of these gory rites. Was it their own free will, or was it compulsion? We know that young savages bear cruel tortures with pride and stoicism, as, for instance, in the often terrible initiation ceremonies. Captain Cook, in his *Voyages*, reported seeing two five-year-old boys in the Tonga Islands fighting desperately for the honour of losing a finger in memory of a chief recently dead.

Finally it is worth recording that most of the hand-prints at Gargas come from small hands. This fact will surprise those who still believe that the first men were a race of giants. As a matter of fact, it has been found by the study of fossilized skeletons that the human race has scarcely changed since the dawn of its existence. We are thus led to wonder whether the hands at Gargas are not those of women or adolescents.

The question has already been raised by Count Begouen in connexion with the prehistoric footprints found in the plastic clay of the caverns of Audoubert and Montespan.

The pieces of the whole puzzle are still few and confused, but what we have learned about prehistory in the past fifty years encourages one to hope for more and more astonishing discoveries concerning the minds of our early ancestors.

PART THREE

EXTINCT ANIMALS

*

Just when a species has reached the height of its power, either in bodily
size or in weapons offensive or defensive, and thus seems safe against all
enemies, that species is invariably on the verge of disappearance

DEPÉRET, *Les Transformations du monde animal*

I

THE GREAT CAVE BEAR OF THE PYRENEES

*

Specus erant pro domibus

*

AT the end of the tertiary and quaternary era what is to-day
France was subjected now to a tropical, now to a polar climate
at the whim of the ice. Each advance of the glaciers drove out
those animals which dislike cold, and brought in polar species.
At each recession of the ice certain animals moved northward,
giving way to African varieties.

The country was the scene of great migrations. In hot
periods the southern elephant, Merck's rhinoceros, the hippopotamus, the sabre-toothed tiger, and, among smaller animals,
the hyena, the porcupine, and monkeys succeeded one another.
When the glaciers advanced, there were bison, horses, stags,
saiga-antelopes, wolves, lions, and tigers. Finally, at the
height of the glacial epoch, in a climate like that of modern
Lapland, there were the mammoth, the woolly rhinoceros, the
reindeer, the musk-ox, the glutton (a sort of wolverine), and
others.

Of these animals, some are extinct, like the mammoth, Merck's and the woolly rhinoceros, the southern elephant, and the sabre-tooth. Others, such as the reindeer, fled thousands of years ago to northern countries, while the hippopotamus, the lion, and most varieties of tiger have established themselves in the hot regions.

Alone among the large animals the bear never emigrated, and still exists in France. This survival and this adaptation to climate are due partly to the fact that the bear, in one species or another, is distributed throughout the earth. No other large wild animal is represented in both polar regions and tropics. The white bear and the Malay bear are but the extremes.

On the other hand – and here is the real reason – the bear, a mountain-dweller, has been able to find a suitable climate by mere change of altitude. In glacial periods the bear lived at the foot of the mountains, and it met warmer ages by a few hours' uphill march, while the migrations of other animals took years.

The bear still haunts the Pyrenees, and, in fact, is commoner there than is generally supposed. The sole French survivor of the great beasts of the quaternary is the brown bear (*Ursus arctos*), of which there are eighteen varieties distributed throughout the world. At the beginning of the quaternary era it had a strong and ferocious relative, now extinct, the great cave bear, or *Ursus spelaeus*.

Cave bears once existed in stupendous number. There is hardly a palaeontological collection in France without its complete skeleton of *Ursus spelaeus*, and nothing short of seeing a skeleton gives any idea of the animal.

It attained the size of a bull, but the bones of an ox look fragile compared to a cave bear's. Its muscles must have been huge, judging by the muscular insertions of the bones; its canine teeth were the size of bananas. When full-grown it was ten feet long, and reached a height of five feet at the shoulder. Its thick hair must have made it seem even bigger.

The cave bear's physical structure was that of the modern brown bear, except that it had no premolar teeth, and that its

The Charnel-House

9

Into the Chasm

Underground Passages

More Underground Passages

Norbert Casteret with his Mother and Wife

Ice Column

13

Western Entrance to the Grotte Casteret

Climbing the Snow Ridge

An Icy Bath on Monte Perdido

Underground Ice

16

forehead was strongly convex, whereas other bears have a receding forehead.

We find most of the bones and complete skeletons of *Ursus spelaeus* in caves – sometimes in great numbers. The bones lie pell-mell among other animal remains, all covered with clay mud which has been washed into the caverns. The fact that the skeletons are often found with bones all in position indicates that the bears lived in the deep caverns, and retired there to die.

I have had some chances, not only to study the skeletons, but to learn curious habits of the huge beasts. Often, although the bones of bears are plentiful, one will find no rubbish from their meals. This means that they devoured their prey in the open air. Secure in their enormous strength, they did not feel obliged to eat underground. The hyenas' lairs, on the other hand, are veritable charnel-houses.

Every spelaeologist knows that *Ursus spelaeus* did not merely shelter in caverns against weather and daylight. It penetrated to great depths, exploring the most out-of-the-way crannies. In fact, the depths of the caverns, far from the easily accessible galleries, are the very places where I have had most luck in tracing the bears' comings and goings.

The bear's five strong, non-retractile claws have left imprints in the plastic clay of the caverns – traces impressive for both their size and their antiquity. Even in narrow vertical passages, where one can climb only by hitching oneself up like a chimney-sweep, I have been surprised to find bear traces on walls covered with clay or delicate stalagmite. Sometimes long scratches tell of desperate efforts and dangerous slides; sometimes, too, I have found skeletons at the foot of pits or steep walls.

In the cavern of Planque (Haute-Garonne), 230 feet below ground, I found the skeletons of two bears which had fallen into one of the lower pits with vertical walls, and which died of hunger after violently scratching the rock in attempts to climb out.

At the Trois-Frères, Count Begouen, discoverer and proprietor of the cavern, always shows his guests the skeletons

UE–3

of an *Ursus spelaeus* and a cub which tried to explore a narrow cavity at the end of the cavern, remained prisoners, and died miserably.

The famous oubliettes of the cavern of Gargas were a trap where many bears perished on their subterranean rounds. There is some doubt at Gargas, however, because dead animals may conceivably have been washed down by the torrential streams which have periodically swept the lower parts of the cavern. Be that as it may, the oubliettes of Gargas are a mine of bears' bones; the great museums procured their finest specimens there.

Eleven hundred yards from the entrance to the cavern of Montespan the bears noticed a narrow gallery opening ten feet above the water. Thanks to their great size they were able to put their forepaws in the opening, but a layer of soft clay makes the place peculiarly difficult to climb into.

Nothing could be more curious and striking than the many long scratches in the clay, which show the bears' obstinate attempts to hoist themselves into the tunnel. We can imagine the beasts falling back heavily into the water, growling as they got up to try again. Some of them succeeded in entering the corridor, which grows smaller after fifty feet. Here their size prevented them from going further, and they clawed up the earth.

The tunnel ends in an impassable crack after a hundred feet. At the end of this cul-de-sac a cub, which can have been no bigger than a poodle, has left the marks of its little claws on the floor.

It is not surprising that the cub continued to explore the tunnel beyond the point where its parents were halted, but the amusing thing, which sheds a light on the animals' habits, is that the cub could not have climbed into the high tunnel alone. Its mother must have strained every nerve to hoist it up. Did she get it to climb on her back? Did she throw or set it in the hole with her paws? More likely she took it in her teeth by the scruff of the neck, perhaps helping it with a shove of paws or nose.

We may wonder how the beasts found their way in the

pitchy dark. Although the cave bear was a nocturnal animal, like the modern Pyrenean bear, it was not really adapted to life underground, as are bats and true cave-dwelling fauna, which have special sense organs. And the blackest night is not comparable to the absolute darkness of the caverns. There seems nothing for it but to suppose that the bears were guided through the caverns by smell and touch alone.

The examples already cited might lead one to believe that the beasts were lost in the labyrinths, desperately looking for an exit. But the bears did not get lost; they enjoyed the caverns. Being of a playful disposition, they actually amused themselves, sometimes quite wildly.

The cavern of the Tuc d'Audoubert has innumerable bear tracks. Toward the bottom of the immense cavern is a chamber, terminated by a sharp clay slope, which once plunged into a small pond. At present the basin is dry, and contains nothing but a mass of clay, but the clay of the slope and of the pond bottom have recorded with perfect distinctness one of the oddest habits of the cave bear.

Count Begouen and his sons have very rightly christened this spot 'the bears' toboggan slide.' The animals took advantage of the slope to go coasting, landing, unhurt, in the muddy water. Some of the tracks show the hairs of the fur in the plastic clay.

This game is familiar to white bears, and polar explorers have often seen them amuse themselves by sliding down ice slopes into the sea. Seals are also tireless in their devotion to the sport.

This diversion is so indispensable to the white bear that Hagenbeck's famous zoo at Hamburg has installed a wooden chute at the bear pool. The chute of the Tuc d'Audoubert was not so perfect, of course, since one had to slide on clay into a mud puddle; but in absolute darkness it must have been more exciting! Of course, it is rare to find a cavern so well arranged for the bears as that of the Tuc d'Audoubert, and they were often obliged to be content with more limited diversion.

A bear when bored with solitude or captivity will resort to the bear dance – an exercise which becomes a regular tic. It is neither varied nor graceful. It consists in rocking from side to side, with an accompanying swing of the head.

This innocent pastime occupied an *Ursus spelaeus* in the cave of Pène-Blanque (Haute-Garonne), which opens at an altitude of 3,250 feet in a cliff of Arbas Mountain. During its long hibernation it marked time for hours, as we can see from the many prints of its four paws, one print over another in the clay.

In the grotto of Tourtoise (Ariège), which is of very broken character, and in the Tuc d'Audoubert, there are two spots almost exactly alike – rugged walls covered with a spongy stalagmitic deposit which the bears have scratched in all directions – partly, we may suppose, to pass the time, partly to sharpen their claws. The claws, of course, not being retractile, constantly got dull from walking.

In many caverns the rock walls and roof of small tunnels have been highly polished by the passing of the bears. Sometimes the bears scratched themselves on projections in the wall, or on short, squat stalagmites like that in the cavern of Girosp (Haute-Garonne), which have preserved a high polish. I may seem to exaggerate when I speak of the bears' polishing the rock, but the reader will remember the stone steps worn by feet, the shine on statues kissed by pilgrims, or even the trees and corners rubbed bright by cattle.

We know that prehistoric man was much occupied and preoccupied with the bear. The terrible beasts were plentiful, and primitive men often battled with them over some underground refuge. What awful dramas must have taken place in the light of smoky torches! The frail weapons of man can have triumphed but rarely.

His bitter struggles and his intimacy with the bear inspired the cave man to produce a few works of art, though it is surprising how few, and of what uneven interest and value. We must probably explain the scarcity of bears in prehistoric art by some magical taboo. The few depictions of bears which do exist were plainly the work of witch-doctors specially authorized to draw the accursed creature.

The first engraving representing a bear was on a pebble

found by Dr Garrigou in the Pyrenean Grotte de Massat (Ariège), and now in the museum at Foix. The design is naïve but very realistic. It shows the animal rising a little on its hind legs, in a menacing attitude, emphasized by a very aptly rendered expression of ferocity. The artist has even scratched great claws, ill-drawn but prominently accentuated.

From the Grotte de Massat come a large number of *Ursus spelaeus* bones. The engraved pebble was in the right place.

Prehistoric engravings of the cave bear

There is another engraving in the cavern of Marsoulas. It is only a full-face sketch of a head, but it shows astonishing observation. The characteristic shape and position of the ears, in particular, indicate that the artist vividly remembered meeting a bear face to face. A drawing almost similar, but even more lifelike, is engraved on a reindeer antler found in the Grotte de Massat by the scholar Édouard Lartet. It is now in the Toulouse Museum.

In the cavern of the Trois-Frères, already so often mentioned, there are three bear drawings on the rock. But here some puzzling magical rite has caused their disfigurement; one of them has a bison's tail and the spots of a leopard or hyena.

The little head of a brown bear carved in rock found by M. Passemard in the grotto of Isturitz (Basses-Pyrénées) deserves attention. The head is treated as a round embossment, and it is a marvel of verisimilitude. The crafty eye is offset by smiling lips and muzzle, giving the face that deceptive air of good nature so characteristic of the bear.

Though made with less art, the clay statue from Montespan

Further bear engravings

undoubtedly remains the most curious and suggestive depiction of the bear, for it brings to life the cave man's desperate struggle with the terror of the caverns.

Besides being the object of incantations, the cave bear was of practical use to the cave man. The capture of a bear was a happy event, undoubtedly accompanied by great rejoicing. It meant plentiful succulent meat, a precious supply of grease, strong tendons, warm luxurious fur, and glorious hunting trophies.

This question of hunting trophies was very important in

prehistoric times; the custom has been universal from the fierce Fijian head-hunter to the peaceable Nimrod who sticks a partridge-feather in his hat. A necklace of claws and canine teeth from bears killed in the hunt decorated the chest of the daring captor. The ornament, of course, was a sign of valour, and it must also have been a precious talisman for future hunts. Ethnography tells us that he who has conquered an enemy or an animal becomes invulnerable by his victory.

The claws, of course, have not survived, but bears' canine teeth, engraved and drilled for stringing, are often found among prehistoric remains.

The teeth which lent distinction to the hunter's outfit did not always come from hand-to-hand combat. We know, definitely, that men sometimes pulled teeth from skeletons found in caves. The famous Tuc d'Audoubert cavern gives proof that there were grave-robbers among the cave men. On the upper level are several skeletons of bears who retired there to die. One of the skulls lacks the canines, which were knocked out by breaking the jaw with a stone. The soft clay beside the skull still bears imprints of the hands, feet, and knees of a man who crouched as he worked. Max Begouen even found a flint blade which the Magdalenian grave-robber had dropped.

It is ridiculous to say, as some popular scientific books do, that man exterminated the cave bear. All the valour of man, even backed up by a belief in infallible spells, could not have destroyed the great beast, but, providentially, nature performed the task, with a swift completeness well calculated to convince men that their curses had taken effect.

Man could never have exterminated the cave bear or any other large animal of that era. He may have caught mammoths in pitfalls, slaughtered bison and horses by ingenious battues, and killed bears by surprise, but this is not why they disappeared. The cause is a law of nature, known, but not yet understood, which regulates species grown too numerous or arrived at the top limit of their size.

No one knows just why the giant reptiles of the secondary era suddenly vanished: no one can explain the extinction of

mastodons and mammoths. *Ursus spelaeus* seems to have succumbed to a disease, for no migration can be traced. In the
present state of palaeontological knowledge we cannot tell the
cause of the disease; we can only see its effects, and state that
the cave bear had disappeared when the great cold of the
Magdalenian epoch brought the reindeer down to the Pyrenees.

So far we have studied the bear 'on the hoof', relying on
such trustworthy records as its skeleton, its footprints, and
contemporary pictures. But when we come to its disappearance we can depend only on reasoned interpretation of
certain remains in sketching the following theory, which I
give as the most likely.

The greatest extension of the glaciers took place in the
middle of the Magdalenian era. This was the longest and
coldest of all the glaciations, and the reindeer abounded in
France, while such mountain animals as the chamois and the
wild goat came down to the plains.

Ursus spelaeus had resisted earlier glacial ages, but this last
great cold was so intense that the bears could not survive
without migrating. Their sedentary instinct kept them from
moving, and they died in great numbers on the frozen earth,
as did more migratory animals surprised by the cataclysm.
Later, the water from melting glaciers swept innumerable
carcasses into the caverns, where they are now found em-
bedded in clay and breccia.

But not all the bears perished alike: some fled deeper than
ever into the caverns, where they found an even, moderate
temperature. This was their way of escaping the mortal cold.
But it was not enough; they had to come out to hunt, and
game was rare in the icy desert. Besides, the penetrating
damp of the caverns caused a degenerative disease, whose
stages are strikingly shown by the monstrous lesions of the
bones found in the caverns.

The Museum of Natural History at Toulouse has a probably
unique collection of diseased bear bones from the Pyrenean
caverns. There are deformed jaws, joined vertebrae, shoulder
blades encrusted with bony tumour, long bones distorted by
a sort of arthritis and sometimes grown together (the two

bones of the lower foreleg). In my private collection is a skull to which the first cervical vertebra is attached by ossification. We can imagine the sufferings caused by such lesions; the animal could neither walk nor hunt, and must soon have died.

This degeneration seems also to have induced the sterility of the individuals affected.

The skeletons of very young cubs are often found below ground, but their bones show no trace of the adult diseases; they succumbed to the crisis caused in large carnivorous animals by teething.

The cold, the arthritis, and the lack of food sealed the doom of the cave bear. The time had to come when the last of the race, crippled by the pitiless malady, dragged his way into some remote tunnel to die.

2

THE CAVE HYENA

*

To a truly philosophical mind, everything is
equally worth knowing
RENAN, *Mélanges d'histoire et de voyages*

*

AMONG the animals with which man disputed the caverns,
the hyena was, without doubt, the least dangerous. But even
the hyena was wily, ferocious, and far from negligible.

The cave hyena frequented certain particular caverns,
where quantities of its bones and fossilized excrements occur.
If the beast was a dangerous and unpleasant neighbour to the
cave man, palaeontologists curse it also, for the hyena made
complete prehistoric skeletons rare. The cave hyena, like its
modern descendants, had such jaws and teeth that not even
the lion and tiger could compete with it in grinding large
bones. And not content with cracking the bones of every
carcass that came in its way, the hyena was equipped to
swallow and digest them.

The digestive waste has accumulated in the hyena caves in
the form of coprolites, or fossilized dung. It is perfectly preserved by its high lime content, due to the phosphates in the
digested bones. Dogs also produce some white coprolites,
which were long used for the preparation of hides in tanning.

The cave hyenas were voracious scavengers; they spared
not even their own dead relatives. There are but two hyena
skeletons in France. One of them is in the famous exhibit of
quaternary animals at the Paris Museum of Natural History,
and the other in the Hall of Caves in the Natural History
Museum at Toulouse. Even here, a few small bones as
ankle-bones, knee-caps, and tail vertebrae had to be borrowed
from modern hyenas to complete the skeletons. Both skeletons

come from the famous Gargas cavern, and were found by Félix Regnault, who began digging there in 1880.

The Paris and Toulouse skeletons survived in a perpendicular abyss sixty-five feet deep (one of the oubliettes of Gargas), which opens treacherously inside the cave; here other hyenas could not reach and devour them. The two skeletons were protected from the destructive effects of air by a thick clay gangue.

Dangerous as the cave hyena's bold thefts, and perhaps its attacks, may have been, it scarcely interested primitive hunters. They could neither hope to exterminate so plentiful a pest nor use the inedible flesh and coarse hair.

It is a certain sign of man's indifference and contempt for these repellent creatures that prehistoric depictions of the hyena are extremely rare. Of all the life of the epoch, the hyena is the animal least often shown. The best specimen is in the Musée des Eyzies (Dordogne) – an ivory statuette from the famous rock shelter of La Madeleine. The head is low and menacing, the legs bent. The statuette realistically reproduces a posture common to this strong but cowardly and treacherous animal.

Another depiction of a hyena, otherwise inferior to the statuette, is remarkable as the smallest rock engraving known. This is the one I discovered at the end of the prehistoric gallery at Montespan. It cannot be examined except by lying flat on one's back, which perhaps explains, and certainly excuses, the bad draughtsmanship.

3

THE MAMMOTH

*

It was 20,000 years ago. On the plains of Europe the
mammoth neared extinction. . . .
J.-H. ROSNY, *Vamireh*

*

THE mammoth (*Elephas primigenius*) is the best known of all
prehistoric animals; it belongs to the elephant family, which
also includes two other extinct lines. To describe the animal
is unnecessary; its picture is universally familiar. I confine
myself here to correcting some wrong ideas of its size and
appearance.

The size of the mammoth, like that of most prehistoric
animals and of primitive man, has always been exaggerated in
the popular mind, which likes to think of contemporary
species as degenerate pygmies.

Though it is true that some modern animals once were
larger and stronger (which in itself proves not degeneration
but adaptation and specialization, which is to say, evolution),
the reverse is true just as often. It is definitely established that
the further back one traces a species, the smaller it becomes,
sometimes to an incredible degree.

For instance, the moeritherium, the common ancestor of
the elephants, was a very small mammal which lived at the
beginning of the tertiary era.

It is not uncommon to read that the mammoth attained a
height of twenty feet, but the exaggeration is evident, for all
the skeletons show that the mammoth was no taller than the
modern elephant. We may take from nine feet nine inches to
ten feet five inches as an average. The maximum is ten feet ten
inches for the famous Indian elephant Jumbo, and ten feet

eight inches for the mammoth skeleton of Baulou (Ariège), the largest known, now in the Foix Museum.

Another error, less glaring, but perhaps more serious (since the naturalists themselves were guilty of it up to a few years ago), was that of drawing the mammoth, and even of mounting its skeleton, with the spine almost horizontal. But it was noticed, not too long ago, that the mammoth's rump was much lower than its shoulders, so that its spine sloped sharply, like a giraffe's. Of course, this gave the animal a very different silhouette – one which seems always to be associated with great walking ability. If the mammoth were still living, and could be domesticated, we certainly could not saddle it like an Indian elephant with a palanquin.

In this respect the African elephant, with its sloping spine, resembles the mammoth. But we must not think that the mammoth bore any other resemblance to the African elephant. The latter has huge ears as fans and fly-chasers, while the mammoth's ears were even smaller than those of the Indian elephant. Modern elephants' tusks are parallel and not much curved, while those of the mammoth were larger, and spread out almost in spirals.

Elephas primigenius possessed yet other peculiarities. The living representatives of the family have thick, bare skins, sprinkled with occasional hairs; the mammoth wore a long, thick fleece of matted reddish wool and black hair, particularly long at the neck, where it formed a luxuriant mane reaching to the knees.

It is hardly necessary to remark that the above statements come from observation of the marvellously preserved mammoths' bodies found in the Siberian ice within living memory. The mammoth and the woolly rhinoceros are the only fossil animals whose bodies have been found frozen in such perfect preservation that it was possible to analyse their blood, study their cells under the microscope, and examine the contents of their stomachs. The mammoth's stomach habitually contained a stupendous quantity of fir shoots.

The Eskimos, who often found the bodies of mammoths long before the scientific world grew excited over them, regarded such a find as a great windfall; they used the fat, and fed the meat to their dogs. What palaeontological treasures have thus been lost to science!

It is true that the members of a scientific congress at St Petersburg in 1905 were more voracious than the Eskimos; at the final banquet they had the whim of eating frozen mammoth steak.

As yet no one knows in what quarter of the globe the mammoth originated, or where it became extinct; but it definitely lived in Europe, Asia, and North America. The oldest remains are found in English tertiary deposits. The most recent are in the lower terraces of quaternary alluvial deposits along European rivers, and in certain caverns, whither they were dragged by carnivorous animals and men.

The caverns, on the whole, furnish few mammoth remains. Mammoths were too big for the hyenas to drag in their bones, and even man must have been content to hack off flesh, leaving the carcass where it lay.

The mammoth, the largest of his contemporaries, cannot but have captured the imagination of the cave man. This we could guess, but we actually know it. In 1864 Larter and Christy found, in the cavern of La Madeleine (Dordogne), an ivory fragment with a superb engraving of a mammoth.

Superb is not too strong a word for this sketch, which would do honour to the best artists of to-day. The Magdalenian engraver has taken little pains with the finish of his 'charging mammoth', but has concentrated on rendering the impact, the irresistible force of the enraged animal. This masterpiece also shows characteristics of the mammoth which were ignored at first, but were later noticed in the frozen Siberian mammoths: tusks extremely curved, trunk fleshier than that of living elephants, small ears, retreating forehead, pointed skull rising above the sloping line of the back, hairy body, abundant mane, long tail.

Since the charging mammoth many depictions have been found, engraved and carved on bone, ivory, pebbles, and drawn and painted on cavern walls. Among the best works is the mammoth carved in reindeer antler from the rock shelter of Bruniquel (Tarn-et-Garonne). With facile originality the artist has shaped the massive mammoth into a dagger handle. The cave of the Combarelles and that at Bernifal, near the Eyzies, contain wall engravings of mammoths.

Finally, one of the most remarkable recent discoveries bearing on the mammoth is that of a veritable mammoth-cemetery at Vistonice (Moravia). In a small area are gathered the remains of more than fifty mammoths, mingled with reindeer and horse bones and traces of human habitation. Here a statuette of a mammoth was found, carved in mammoth tusk.

Prehistoric art, countless bones, and, above all, the frozen bodies at the mouth of the Lena have combined to make the mammoth one of the most studied animals of prehistoric times. It has long been the one with the greatest hold on popular imagination.

4

THE EUROPEAN BISON

*

There is perhaps no migration of quadrupeds more beautiful than the
bison's journey across the plains
CHATEAUBRIAND, *Le Génie du christianisme*

*

THE last survivor of the great animals of the quaternary in
Europe, the European bison, having outlived the mammoth,
the woolly rhinoceros, and the cave bear, having seen the
extinction, at the beginning of this century, of the clumsy
saiga-antelope, is threatened with extinction in its turn. Just
after World War I the last specimens in the mysterious
Russian forest of Byalowiska, formerly protected by the Tsar,
died out, and the species was believed extinct, but a few still
proved to exist in the central Caucasus. It is a different variety,
but close enough to the Byalowiska bison – the *Bonassus
caucasicus*.

The European bison is a close relative of the American
buffalo, from which it differs in having a more slender
appearance, considerably greater stature (up to five feet ten
inches at the shoulder), a lighter colour, less luxuriant mane,
and much less conspicuous hump. The European bison, in
fact, is one of the largest mammals on earth. The study of
bone remains shows that the surviving bison is considerably
smaller than its prehistoric ancestor.

There can be no doubt that the European bison, like its
American cousin, was originally a steppe-dweller and a great
wanderer. Prehistoric caverns from Russia to Spain contain
innumerable bones. Huge herds of bison made long migrations
with the seasons, perhaps with the glaciers. So did the mammoth, the rhinoceros, the saiga-antelope, the horse, the reindeer, and their ancient and implacable enemies, man and the
wolf.

Despite the bones which clutter the prehistoric hearths in some caverns, no museum has a complete skeleton of *Bos primigenius*. This no doubt is because the bison did not frequent caves, and its remains can have been only dragged there by man and a few carnivores. And the bison, like the mammoth, was too big to haul into a cave entire.

When we further consider that our ancestors cracked and crushed all the long bones to get at the precious marrow, we can well understand why intact osteological remains are rare.

Under certain exceptional circumstances we need not yet give up hope of discovering a complete skeleton. The conditions exist in certain abysses or natural wells, huge traps on whose bottoms lie the skeletons of animals which have fallen in in the course of ages. The cavern of the Trois-Frères has such a shaft. From the great heap of rubbish at the bottom Count Begouen and his sons dig out more bones every year, among them those of a bison which they have partly reconstructed, and which they hope eventually to complete.

One thing which we can see from all the bones is the importance of the bison in the diet, crafts, art, and religion of the Stone Age tribes.

The gluttonous feasts held by our ancestors at the expense of the bison are vividly recalled by incredible accumulations of broken and charred bones. Thrown pell-mell among this kitchen debris are divers instruments – domestic, warlike, symbolic – shaped out of the bone.

Bone engravings of the bison are many and varied. We can say that, along with horse and reindeer, the bison was man's chief interest in life, his hope, his joy, and his care. When the bison was plentiful, there was wealth and celebration; its rarity meant mortal cold and terrible famine. If we can speak of the age of steam or electricity, we may also speak of the bison age.

The cave engravings and paintings alone would justify this statement. Bisons abound in the caves. They are shown wounded with arrows, spears, hatchets, and stones. They were all drawn, as we know, to assure the success of the hunt.

The most curious practice is shown by the clay bisons

already described in the Tuc d'Audoubert. For some reason the bison must at that time have been absent from the Pyrenees, at least from the hunting-grounds of the Tuc d'Audoubert cave-dwellers. This disappearance of their favourite game must have produced consternation, and induced the tribe to make the symbolic clay figures, with appropriate incantations to assure multiplication of the species.

PART FOUR

UNDER GROUND

*

Regna solitudinis

I

MY FIRST CAVERN

*

Et quocumque viam dederit fortuna sequamur
VERGIL

*

I AM not talking here of my very first cavern, the modest grotto of Bacuran in the gorges of the Save (Comminges), which I saw at the age of five with my parents by torchlight, nor of the insignificant caves of L'Escalère, at Saint-Martory, where I went during the long vacations to rob hawks' nests and read *Le Roi des montagnes* on the airy crags mirrored in the green flood of the Garonne. No doubt those dizzy ledges whetted my appetite for adventure and exploration, but they could not satisfy it. What I wanted was caverns. I wanted to penetrate the very bowels of the earth.

One day, while rummaging through a case of books in my father's attic, I found a slender work with pages still uncut, the very title of which made me feel like a bibliophile with a Forty-two-line Bible. The pamphlet was called *The Hyenas' Lair in the Cavern of Montsaunès*, and it told me that less than two miles away there was a grotto I did not know of. From this note to the Natural History Society of Toulouse I learned that about 1890 a scholar by the name of Édouard Harlé (all of whose works I have since read) had done some palaeontological digging at the mouth of the cavern, and had found various animals' bones brought in by a pack of hyenas. And what bones – elephant, hippopotamus, wolf, beaver, porcupine, even a monkey's jaw! The report spoke of 'tropical fauna', going back to the warm, damp period at the beginning of the quaternary era, to the fabulous epoch which saw the last of many great animals and the first appearance of man on earth.

Harlé had not explored the rest of the cavern.

Of course I was far from understanding all the scientific ideas of the monograph, but one thing I took unto myself: there was a partly unexplored cavern close by, containing hyena skeletons and remains of 'antediluvian' animals. With juvenile enthusiasm I grabbed a candle and matches, leaped on my bicycle, and hurried off to the Montsaunès quarry where the cavern was. A chance blast twenty-five years before had uncovered the mouth of the gallery.

I rushed madly into the artificial semicircle of the quarry, but had taken only a few steps when I was loudly challenged and pursued by three old quarry-workers. Their day was finished, and they had been quietly packing the dynamite whose explosion was to furnish the morrow's work. I had rushed in just as they were about to light the fuse!

I retreated to a neighbouring field, where an old woman was herding her sheep. Full of my idea of exploring the cavern, I tried to get some information from the shepherdess. She was very old, and I was very young, and instead of the facts I wanted, I had the privilege of hearing one of the prettiest of the fairy-tales current about the caves of the Pyrenees.

After the blasts, I waited until the surly quarry-workers had left. It was dusk of a lovely day, and the quarry was still and lonely; a blackbird complained of my unaccustomed presence. Flat on my stomach, with beating heart, I crawled into my first real cavern. It was the dry bed of an underground watercourse, and I had to crawl on the soft clay bottom. The cool air, the damp soil, and soundless blackness made a striking contrast with the world outside. They created an atmosphere of their own. I was entering another, a mysterious world,

which scared me at the same time that it filled me with a
mystical enthusiasm.

The cavern had been hollowed out by the elements in the
course of geologic ages. Remains of animals now gone from
the earth gradually piled up in it. Packs of hyenas followed.
An underground stream, following in turn, covered all the
bones with mud and gravel; then it, too, dried up and vanished.

Lying on my stomach, candle in hand, eyes searching the
gloom, I felt myself a new Argonaut on the brink of an unknown world, trying to pierce the darkness of the past. After
a stretch of painful wriggling I was able to walk stooping,
and then to stand up in a corridor where I put to flight an
unsuspected inhabitant. I had a moment's bad fright before I
recognized it as a startled rabbit.

Further along, the floor dropped away into a funnel
occupying the whole width of the gallery; the cavern went on
straight and horizontal beyond. I threw in a few pebbles,
which bounced into the depths and were swallowed up. By
an acrobatic feat, nerve-tingling to a novice in such absolute
isolation, I managed to pass the pit. I went on to a second deep
funnel.

From this rose a new sound, since grown familiar to my
ears – the murmur of a brook in an unknown lower level.
Surprise and delight riveted me to the spot. Since then I have
swum countless icy torrents below ground, but I still fondly
remember my first, the humble rivulet of Montsaunès.

I had entered the cave at twilight. Darkness must be falling
outside, and people would be worried about me. Besides, I
had but one candle. Casting a last look at the gallery, which
went invitingly on ahead, I turned back.

Next day I was at the cavern mouth with my young brother
Martial at an even later hour than before. We had picked the
time so as to dodge the quarry-workers, who might have kept
us out of the cave. And I must admit that an expedition at
night had its charms for me anyway. Both starry nights and
underground gloom have always fascinated me, and the combination was irresistible.

We crouched at the mouth of the grotto to light our candles.

I shouldered a boy-scout knapsack containing a rope, a hammer, and a package of candles, and crawled into a narrow hole, followed by my agile and determined brother. In a few minutes we reached and crossed the second funnel, which was too small for us to descend. Soon we found some crystals. The bare and muddy earth began to give way to a limestone floor covered with formations; then we were in a grotto full of stalactites. These strange stone shapes were entirely new to us, and we wandered ecstatically from white, pointed stalactite to brown, stumpy stalactite, admired a petrified cascade, and then pushed on into the cavern, which we enthusiastically made our own.

We got past several pits like the first one. At the bottom we kept hearing the brook on the lower level, where our imagination ran ahead of us. But suddenly, just as our horizontal march promised to go on indefinitely, a chasm halted us. It was no simple funnel which could be stepped over or passed on a ledge; it cut off the cavern completely, with no yonder edge and no visible corridor beyond. The near edge was rounded like a helmet, and covered with slippery clay, so that we could not get near enough to judge the depth. Very handily, there was a limestone column on the spot, joining floor and ceiling. We knotted our forty-foot rope firmly to the column, and, after throwing in some stones to learn the approximate depth of the hole, I fastened my lighted candle to my hatband, and slid down the rope.

It was my first descent, and in what a rustic outfit! It was also my first shiver, but a short one, for I quickly touched bottom. Still quivering from this exploit, I shouted orders and advice to my brother, who descended in turn, peppering me with lumps of clay as he slid. Suddenly, while his boots were dangling above my head and I was about to receive him at arms' length, a sizzling was heard, with a frightful smell of something burning. In my excitement I had forgotten the candle on my hat, and the hat had caught fire! I flung it from me. My brother, doubled up with laughter, dropped on me from above.

The punctured hat of Montsaunès has been in many a

cavern since, and the subject of many a joke. It has become as legendary to us as the great felts of the Gascon Cadets, 'whose plumes hide the holes.'

Mastering our laughter, we put our minds on getting forward. We had a choice of directions. At the very foot of the wall was a sort of steep air-hole, while on the other side the cavern went on as a corridor larger and more rugged than the one we had left behind. We were in a hurry to find the underground brook, so we preferred the muddy sluice to the open corridor.

I wriggled into the hole head first. My body was tightly squeezed, and I got ahead only because of the slope and the slippery clay. With arms stretched forward I alternately hastened and braked my descent by appropriate wrigglings.

Suddenly my hands plunged into water so clear it was invisible. Of course, the candle went out, and there was I in the dark, like a pea in a pea-shooter, my wrists gripped by cold-water bracelets. My brother might have been able to extricate me by my feet from the trap, but I was encouraged by the shallow water and by an enlargement of the tunnel which I had glimpsed, so I continued to coast. Dragging myself by my hands, and then on all fours, I soon splashed blindly into the brook-bed. My brother joined me, pushing the knapsack before him. This was how we reached our goal, the brook – so clear and at that point so quiet that only its chilly embrace betrayed its presence.

Quite apart from the excitement, this expedition taught us fundamental lessons; it was a regular model of cavern formation, of nature at work.

We walked for a long time in a dark tunnel, following the Ariadne's thread of the brook; we were led on from rock to rock, from basin to cascade, up to a last narrow crevice. Here the spell was broken. The water plunged into the fissure, and deserted us with a sound like a sob. This was the end of the practicable cavern.

At midnight, after exploring the entire lower level, we were back at the bottom of the wall. We tested our rope, the slender link between us and the world. Then we decided to look into the tunnel we had not yet tried. Here we learned that sticky mud can be an insuperable obstacle. We battled nobly with butterlike walls and slopes; after a few yards' hard-won ascent we would slide back in a mass of clay. By giving each other a leg-up we conquered several slopes, to find ourselves in a rock corridor full of immaculate stalactites. We were sheer chunks of clay, our fingers stuck together with mud, and we had trouble in keeping the mud-covered candles alight. We were forced to stop and scrape ourselves with our knives.

The gallery was spiked with stalactites and stalagmites. It grew narrower, and the roof gradually sank. Once more we had to crawl. The ceilings still descended, and then went on parallel to the floor, smooth and damp. We negotiated a few yards of this 'clothes-wringer', and then a couple of arms' lengths away I saw the conduit closed by a forest of squat and serried pillars. There was no going on, and probably the cavern ended there.

But we would leave no stone unturned. The hammer came out of the knapsack. I lay flat on my stomach on the wet slope. Confined by the narrow tunnel, I wielded the hammer at arm's length, my cheek glued to the floor. I attacked the grating of limestone pillars with a mowing movement, and the more fragile ones splintered in all directions. My posture was extremely tiring, and the pitiful results irritated me. I flew into a destructive frenzy. Not until I was quite exhausted would I crawl back to make way for my brother. Panting, clinging to the slippery floor, we thought of nothing but the exit which might possibly reward our labour. Each blow well struck, each broken column was greeted with a shout. We worked as desperately as if we had been walled in. Explorers' fever had hold of us, and nothing short of collapse would stop us.

My brother, worn out in his turn, made way for me, and I went at my sapping and mining with renewed frenzy. I found the weak point in the barrier, and little by little the breach widened, while the heap of broken stalactites grew. A lucky hammer-blow shattered a thick bar of limestone. Through the loophole I could see the continuation of the corridor at last, with a rising ceiling. We would make it yet!

Crawling absolutely flat, squeezing and scraping violently between floor and roof, we did indeed manage to get through. We had to hold our breaths and choke back that instinctive, reflex fear of stifling which is the most painful and persistent emotion to be dealt with underground.

Once past the bottle-neck we were astonished and rather uneasy. We had come from a crack so small that there seemed no hope of passing in the other direction. But the cavern went on, and for the moment that was all that mattered. The roof rose, and clay hillocks stood here and there along the gallery; new wells yawned at our feet. We went rapidly onward, avid for the sights and sensations of the unknown.

An obstacle was not long in appearing; difficulties and disappointments are the rule underground. The gallery stopped abruptly. In the end wall was a loophole at about the height of a man. This we immediately assaulted, and found ourselves in a dry tube with a dusty floor where I was dumbfounded to find traces of a small animal. Plainly the creature could not have got into the cavern from the quarry end; all sorts of obstacles barred the way. Then there must be another outlet, and we must be on our way to it. Perhaps within a few yards we should come out in the woods.

The grotto resounded with our surprise and hope.

But just as we were expecting the outlet, and trying to guess how far we had travelled below ground, the tube came to a dead end. In the last three feet of the cavern we found the frail skeleton of a marten. Above our heads the high walls almost touched. The little creature must have left the surface by some network of cracks, and fallen into the cavern to perish miserably.

This was the end, and we had to retrace our steps. At three in the morning we came out of the cavern, muddy and foot-sore, to mount our dewy bicycles. We went home through the sleeping countryside in reflective silence.

2

MY FIRST CHASM

*

It is not necessary to hope in order to try, nor to
succeed in order to persevere
WILLIAM THE SILENT

*

My first chasm – how I dreamed of it! So far I had attacked only those caverns which could be explored with the very simplest outfit – an acetylene lamp, candles, and a forty-foot rope for short descents.

Vertical chasms were beyond me for lack of proper equipment, and I was reduced to poring over Martel's *Les Abîmes*, the only book I then had. The account of his bold and thrilling underground explorations is illustrated with innumerable plans and cuts.

How I dreamed over them! The very names of the chasms made me dizzy, and stimulated a wild desire to imitate the hero of these perilous exploits. Here was a man who descended to terrifying depths to look at underground France, and who discovered the palace of the Thousand and One Nights for the greater glory of science. He thought nothing of risking his life daily by having himself let down on a rope tied to the middle of a stick; he rode his broomstick clad in a bowler hat and a sack coat, like a Jules Verne scientist. É.-A. Martel was 'the man of the chasms', the discoverer of Padirac, of the Aven Armand, of Rabanel, the Mas Raynal, the Baumes Chaudes, and of heaven knows how many other enormous cavities. He has explored hundreds in many countries. Of course, I did not dream that I should have the honour one day of becoming his disciple and friend, and how could I have known that I would discover and give his name to the deepest abyss in France?

Les Abîmes was too fascinating. I could not resist it, and gradually the determination took root: I would go down a chasm.

For want of the indispensable rope ladders, winch, and assistants I had to eliminate a great many pits as too deep. I pitched on a nice 211-foot cavity the plan of which showed that one could get down with 113 feet of rope. The rest was a forty-five-degree slope, with heaps of rubble. Besides, the chasm was in the forest of Arbas, almost at my door. It was in the lower Pyrenees of the Haute-Garonne at an altitude of 2,600 feet.

Somewhat less than twelve and a half miles on my bicycle brought me one fine day to the village of Arbas. I asked an old man about the Gouffre de Planque. Yes, indeed, he knew the chasm, but under another name: Le Poudac Gran – the Great Well. He even remembered a man from Paris who had come to Arbas and rounded up guides, porters, and mules to go tenting on the mountain and descend into the chasms.

I listened eagerly to this man who had seen Martel. He described him picturesquely, and told anecdotes that had been handed down in the village, where Martel's work had caused a sensation.

My luck was in; the old fellow was inexhaustible. But what suspicion and disdain when I revealed my intention of descending the Gouffre de Planque! Mountaineers are proud of their mountains, and unwilling to be outdone in hardihood; the old man changed his tune. By all means let people be interested in the caverns; let them come from afar to inquire about them; that was flattering; but go down in . . . ?

Ill-will and ignorance appeared forthwith: the chasm was the most dangerous in the country, Martel had just missed being killed by an avalanche of stones, and had let down a rope 'sixty *cannes* long' (350 feet) without touching bottom.

I should really have been shaken if I had not had in my note-book the sketch of the chasm drawn by Martel's companions, Rudaux and Jammes, and been accustomed to the exaggerations of peasants describing caverns they have never been in.

I had to pretend humility, and say that I wanted merely to see the opening. This calmed the old fellow enough for him to give me confused directions, interrupted by 'You can't go wrongs' of evil omen. He told me that a two-hour climb through the woods would bring me to the edge of the chasm, 'near a big beech.'

I crossed and recrossed the woods in every direction, looking for the big beech. Finally, by pure luck, I caught sight not of the tree but of a black hole partly masked in leaves. It was the chasm I wanted.

I was panting with fatigue and excitement, for I knew at once that this gaping maw was the Gouffre de Planque. I had read the description until I knew it by heart.

As I slipped off my heavy knapsack I realized with shame and despair that I was no explorer. I would never dare attempt such a chasm – the very sight of it scared me to death.

In the book the picture of the chasm was plain and simple. A sloping well sixty-five feet deep, a perpendicular drop of thirty, and then a great slope of rubble slanting down into a vast chamber, all the way to the bottom. Compared to the reality it all looked imaginary and conventionalized. I was close to believing the old mountaineer against Martel! I was hypnotized by the dizzy plunge of the tunnel, at the mouth of which my recent school learning put the sign, 'All hope abandon . . .'

A slight mist, smelling damply of earth and lichens, wet the moss and the black slippery rock of the slanting tunnel. I seemed to see Dante's condemned souls grimacing as they fell and fell endlessly.

My first impulse was to turn tail, but somehow I felt that I could not go away like this. The noonday bell had long since rung from the valley, and it was time to eat. I was counting on my scanty lunch to refresh me, take my mind off my fears, and give me time to get used to the chasm and to the idea that I had to go down it. Sitting on the edge of the hole, then, I ate my lunch, looking alternately at the black chasm and at the sunlit valley.

The hour had come. I leaped to my feet. I set to work

uncoiling the ropes, and tying them end to end. I had got together all the cordage I could lay hands on, a motley lot. Altogether there were 113 feet of rope, not very suitable because too thin, though it was strong enough for the weight of an adolescent.

The handling of the rope and the tremendous knot with which I tied it to the nearest tree gave me confidence. I kept telling myself to be calm and determined, and immodestly reminding myself of my prowess in games of strength and agility. All this helped to restore my wits. Having got rid of all useless encumbrances, taken a lighted candle in my teeth, and hooked the acetylene lamp to my belt, I was not too much frightened as I backed down hand over hand into the abyss.

At sixty-five feet the forty-five-degree tunnel suddenly ended in a vertical drop, which in fact overhung a little, so that everything was plunged in darkness. It was the delicate point in the descent, but, trusting to my strong arms and Martel's description, I did not hesitate. I knelt backward on the edge of the void, and then dropped on my stomach on the overhang, below which the rope dangled free. As my head passed the ledge, the candle bumped and went out. My vertical descent now was blind and out of reach of the walls. A hundred feet does not look like much in figures, but in reality it is the height of a seven-storey building; on a dangling rope in the dark it seems like more.

It was a happy moment when I touched ground, and relit my candle and then the lamp. I was flushed with pride. I had vanquished my fears, and conquered my first chasm!

In the acetylene light I realized the vastness of the chamber. The roof was so high it was out of sight. The steep, sloping floor was covered with rubbish. I hurried down at once, for I was in a great hurry to reach 211 feet below ground.

As I went down I made two discoveries, both of them fresh and exciting to me. Among countless sheep bones I found a stag's antlers. They must have been extremely old, for the animal has not lived in the Pyrenees within the memory of man. Further on, partly crushed under a boulder, I saw a brown bear's skeleton, the skull quite well preserved.

All these animals had fallen down the sloping tunnel at the top, a regular natural trap, and their skeletons lay there pell-mell. Huge and rotten tree-trunks had also rolled down. Beyond the debris I found a miniature lake, fed by a ridged and petrified stalagmite cascade. A thin film of water brought its lime deposit day by day, and then ran into the crystal-clear basin. The overflow ran down a narrow crack towards heaven knows what distant valley spring.

So this was the bottom of a chasm. In the silence and solitude it was a moving experience thus to surprise the water at work as it dripped from the ceiling and formed the pool. Little springs and great subterranean rivers alike feed on such hidden reservoirs as this.

But I discovered that the reservoir was not fed by the drip from walls and ceiling alone. Water trickled from the great heap of debris; it had rinsed everything, including the carrion. Underground, as everywhere else, bad goes with good, and poison mingles with purity. After such an object-lesson I began to understand Martel's excited and noisy campaigns against the crime of contaminating springs.

I had gone down over the centre of the rubble; along one of the sides, close to the wall, I started back up towards the rope. On the way I noticed a rising tunnel in the wall. I went in, wondering; this vestibule was mentioned neither in the book nor in the plan I had. The rugged tunnel opened into a horizontal grotto with a dusty earth floor. The air was heavy, and sounds were subdued and without echo. At my feet I saw some enormous bones, which I recognized, but which I had never seen except under glass in natural history museums. They were skeletons of the cave bear.

Kneeling, I gathered skulls and jaw-bones with formidable canines. I imagined the bones alive, a group of enormous beasts which made the cavern echo with their growls.

Beyond this hall I found a narrow and broken gallery, sharply interrupted by a drop whose bottom was too deep for my feeble light. Some pebbles which I dropped seemed to fall a very long way. The Gouffre de Planque, it seemed, had been but partially explored; some of its extensions were unknown. And how had the cave bear got in and out? That day I knew the private, heady delight – how familiar since! – of setting foot in an unknown cavern for the first time.

I could go no further for lack of rope. But I soon made a second expedition, armed with a spare rope for the second shaft. With mingled curiosity and fear I slid down into the hole. A candle in my teeth was all the light I had. By swinging the rope I got a foothold on a ledge twenty-five or thirty feet down. This admitted me to a new level of the cavern, where I went cautiously forward, abandoning the shaft as too deep and dangerous for a lone man as ill-equipped as I. On this level I found some more cave-bear skeletons. Finally I was stopped in my tracks by another shaft occupying the whole corridor.

The gallery continued on the further edge of the chasm; its dark vault beckoned on. I pondered a moment before turning back. I saw a way to surmount the new obstacle, and I was in haste to try it out.

A few days later I left my bicycle at the village for the third time. Bent under a knapsack heavier than ever, I started climbing through the forest. I began to fear that the natives might get interested in my doings, and on this particular day I was most anxious not to be noticed.

I lunched as usual at the mouth of the chasm. As I ate I studied some near-by young chestnuts with slender black trunks. Unwrapping a newly sharpened hatchet, I headed for a superb young tree. The fear of a policeman, or rather of a forester, gave me pause as I was about to swing, but not for long. My mind was made up, and my plan was ready. I felt like an amateur cracksman as I attacked the chestnut, which soon toppled quietly. I trimmed the trunk clean in a few seconds, threw the tell-tale branches into the chasm, picked up the chips, covered the cut surface of the stump with moss, and shoved the pole down the sloping shaft. It dropped like a plummet.

A few minutes later – having gone down the rope – I put my tree on my shoulder, and tramped heavily towards the rising tunnel. My long, heavy load was hard to transport up the steep grade; I pushed, pulled, and carried the tree like an ant with a straw. The lantern, though indispensable, was much in the way.

Suddenly I was astounded to see a rat a few yards away, apparently hypnotized by my light. The true cave-dwellers of France (except for bats) are all insects and animalculae; my excitement at finding a rodent here may be imagined. I stared at it face to face; it had extraordinarily prominent whiskers. Was it blind, like the *Neotoma*, the American blind rat of Mammoth Cave? It occurred to me that the creature would be an interesting catch; but, how to get it? I had the lamp in one hand, and the other hand kept the tree on my shoulder. Gently I let go of the trunk, which teetered on my bent back. I grabbed my cap and hurled it at the rat. My aim was good: the rat rolled from its boulder to my feet. But at the same moment the pole fell, half crushing me as it slid backward and crashed down the corridor. It did not stop until it reached the great chamber full of debris. Rubbing my head and back, I picked up my headgear, but the rat had disappeared. I have never seen another cave rat, so I regret this abortive capture the more. Disappointed of the rat, I went after the tree, which had gone so rapidly down the slope where I had painfully dragged it up.

Since that adventure long ago I have done many unexpected things in caverns; I have even gone skating on a frozen underground lake; but I shall never forget taking that heavy, awkward tree-trunk through the winding corridors. Bumping and tugging, I finally reached the edge of the last shaft, where the pole was to be balanced as a bridge. It was a bit too flexible, and airy enough for any one, but it would carry a light weight. I could not cross astride, because the tree was too slender, and would have rolled. I had to use what alpinists call the Tyrolean method, hanging below the bar, and holding on with both hands and one leg.

To say that I was perfectly cool as I travelled head down across the void would be wide of the truth. My lamp on the edge of the shaft was my only witness and my only encouragement. It might also have been the only witness of my last

Mouth of the Cigalère Cave

La Pyramide de Serre and Mouth of the Gouffre Martel (+)

17

The Floor of the Cigalère Cave

Gypsum Flowers

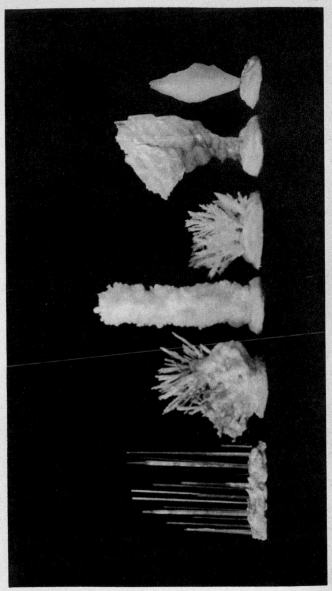

Gypsum Flowers

Ad augusta per angusta

The Frontier Ridge from the Mouth of the Cigalère

Sea of Clouds near the Gouffre Martel

The Electron Rope Ladder

Climbing the Cascades

plunge. But I was as spry as I was foolhardy, and I got across without incident.

On the opposite brink I took a candle from my pocket, lit it, looked back at the lamp and the frail bridge across the chasm, and started at last down the inviting corridor. The corridor turned within a few yards, and came to an end, a blind alley!

It was a sad blow. But one must never give up, below ground least of all. I scratched on the clay floor the words that Rostand put in Cyrano's mouth: 'And it's all the better for being useless' (*Et c'est bien plus beau lorsque c'est inutile*).

3

THE GREAT CAVERN OF CAGIRE

*

All hope abandon, ye who enter here
DANTE, *Inferno*, Canto iii

*

ONE winter evening I was returning from a ski ascent of the Pic de Cagire, that lovely mountain in Comminges. The sun had just set as I coasted down the last slopes. I was about to turn aside towards the village which crouches at the foot of the mountain when my eye fell on a group of trees around a circular depression (called a *doline* in those parts). In limestone country these often betray a sink-hole cut by the water. I went over out of curiosity. Two adjacent funnels yawned under cover of trees and bushes. One of them was blocked a few yards down. The other was a natural well several yards across, its perpendicular sides covered with snow and icicles. I threw down some snowballs, but could not even guess how deep the well might be.

At the village, where I told of my discovery, they assured me that the shaft was very deep – bottomless, in fact – and that the dead animals of the whole countryside were flung down it. I took the liberty of doubting the first statement, but long experience led me to fear that the second was too true.

I put down the shaft in my notes as a place to be explored. Months went by.

One shining May morning I returned. Flowery meadows and thickets filled with bird song had taken the place of winter twilight. The clump of trees and bushes which masked the *doline* was now a leafy nest, the very essence of spring. A blackbird fled at my approach, and a twittering congress of tomtits continued to flirt about. Before, on skis, I had scared a few crows out of the high, bare branches.

At the edge of the hole I opened my bag, and spread on the grass my overall, rope, lantern, candles, and other equipment. I chucked some stones into the shaft to listen for the echo. Then I fastened my rope to a beech trunk, dropped the other end into the void, and went down hand over hand at a good speed, to avoid tremor and fatigue of the arms. I thumped against walls, now rocky, now covered with hart's-tongue fern. Below me the rope jerked violently about, slapping the rock. I soon saw its end whirling under my feet. Having descended sixty-five feet, I made myself fast as alpinists do with two or three turns of rope around the thigh. Then I waited for my eyes to get used to the darkness.

The sounds from above were infinitely faint. I was dangling between two worlds – above me light, warmth, bird song, rustling leaves; below me blackness, cool dampness, the smell of clay and wet rock, the perpetual whisper of dripping water.

This was the threshold of adventure, and I felt the old, irresistible excitement. Fifteen feet below me I saw a platform cluttered with stones, branches, leaves, and carcasses. Was it the bottom of the well? Was it but an outcrop? I should not know the answer that day, for I was at the end of my rope.

The expedition a failure? If you like; but never mind, I would come back with a longer rope. To-day I had bicycled a long way with my equipment on my back, merely to reconnoitre. Like all caverns, the shaft gave me so much to study and think about that I was not disappointed. Besides, exploring alone is my favourite occupation, the most exciting I know. It demands the most absolute self-reliance.

But an end to reflections! The rope tourniquet began to make my leg throb. I released myself, and climbed back to daylight, moving evenly to avoid jerks.

True to an old habit, I was not going to leave without examining the other funnel, whose bottom was visible through the bushes. By arching my back I got through the thicket to the deepest part of the *doline*. It was full of rocks, through which I rummaged, looking for a possible crack. Traces of streams and patches of moss guided my practised eye. There was a crevice, but it was too small to get through.

Trying to clear a tunnel is almost always hopeless. But the huge funnel, the nearness of the other shaft, the nature of the rock, and the looks of the water outlet made me hope to find a big hole under the landslip. I went to work tearing up handfuls of moss, and then patiently dislodging stone after stone from its bed.

For an hour I was intent on my work. I must have looked quite crazy to any one but a cavern-lover.

I struggled long with one boulder which I finally managed to balance out of the way. Below it I found a conduit hollowed from the living rock. The digging was finished, the passage opened, and all danger of a new landslip prevented.

A moment later I had my acetylene lamp in hand, and my pockets empty of anything that might hinder my eel-like progress. The rat-hole into which I was wriggling was a very snug fit.

Very few tubes are impassable if one knows how to crawl (there is an art to it), and dares to keep on, come what may. Thanks to his shape, man can stretch out longer and thinner than any animal of his size.

The stories of people's getting jammed, and dying miserably in narrow passages, are, unfortunately, true. But I believe such accidents start with the awful fear of not being able to get out. This causes one to stiffen up, and to make super-human efforts which soon bring exhaustion. The child who has put his head between the rungs of a chair-back begins to struggle at once, and is injured because he thinks he cannot get loose. He is too frightened to find the position which originally allowed him to push his head through. But agility, gentleness, and sang-froid will get one out of skin-tight tunnels.

Though the small opening made me cautious, then, I was not afraid of it, and I was soon crouching inside the cavern. I could still see daylight where I had got in, but as I looked back the passage seemed absolutely impossible. A narrow corridor went down in the other direction.

Plain traces of erosion marked the course of a stream which must long have poured swiftly down the upper funnel into the rocky conduit where I now was. One of my chief reasons for going below ground is to study the mechanics of subterranean waters. Now that I had found the path of the water, I was eager to see what else I could learn.

The slope of the tunnel was accentuated here and there by drops of several yards – former waterfalls – which I negotiated by ridges and cracks in the walls. Below the third fall I set foot on a mass of gravel brought down by the stream and piled up here in a horizontal corridor.

The water had whirled down the sloping passage, cutting away falls here and there; then the current had abated, depositing the heavier part of its load, and leaving masses of fine mud further on. Starting there, I trod the plastic clay floor characteristic of most caverns. Sometimes these layers of earth reach an unbelievable thickness.

I came to a fork, and chose a side gallery which ended in a cul-de-sac. There was a rapid drip from the funnel-shaped ceiling, however – the remnant of an old stream now largely dead. I went back to the main gallery. It wound capriciously, but its elbows were almost all right angles, corresponding to the natural faults in limestone rock. I passed several small tubes which had once made their contributions to the stream, and then found myself suddenly in a spacious chamber, the main artery of an underground system. It must once have been active and important, drawing off all the surface water from the plateau.

I had scarcely swung my lamp around to get an idea of the gallery when I began to hear sad, shrill little cries. They echoed and multiplied until they were deafening. These lamentations of little creatures lost below ground must be at the bottom of many a fairy tale, many a story of souls in torment.

It was a colony of bats. I could not see them yet, but I was sure they must be very numerous. While I was inspecting the walls and ceiling I slipped in a heap of guano, deceptively like a pile of coffee grounds, but sparkling with fragments of insects' wing-cases. These bats live entirely on insects. Above the guano (possibly centuries old) I soon made out an enormous tawny, silky mat covering the wall like a giant bearskin.

It was a vast crowd of bats, packed like a swarm of bees. I put my hand in to see how deep it was, but the chilly little bodies were tightly jammed. The whole colony (or at least those on the surface) began to be disturbed by my light. The noise increased, heads with huge ears and invisible eyes rose in all directions, wings opened. Suddenly, by what preconcerted signal I cannot say, the whole mass took to flight. The lamp flickered, and I was brushed from head to foot, and enveloped in a puff of warm, musky air. For several minutes the colony whirled about; there was a chorus of cries and fluttering of parchment wings; then the bats dispersed into distant black galleries where no man had ever ventured.

The quick disappearance of the bats was one sign of the cavern's vast extent. I resumed my exploration, carefully strewing the ground with bits of paper, of which I always carry a pocketful. They marked my wanderings in the maze, and assured me of finding the way back. The bat vestibule was floored with earth, and an old brook-bed was channelled through the centre of the clay. I was soon walking in a trench whose sides were higher than my head. The water had cut absolutely vertical, parallel walls; sometimes the descending water-level had produced horizontal benches. It was all strikingly reminiscent of the front-line trenches. At one turn I ran into a natural cylindrical chamber as if for protection against enfilading fire, and a few steps further on was a breach in the parapet just like a machine-gun emplacement.

Suddenly I heard a noise. I stopped and held my breath.

Below ground all one's senses are unreliable. The light is bad, and the acoustics are very peculiar, but making allowance for distortions I recognized the sound of running water. It seemed to be at a great depth. This was quite likely, for almost all large caverns have several levels, and the water follows natural law by abandoning the upper galleries in favour of the lower. The upper levels are but a series of old brook-beds, for ever dead as the water digs deeper.

A few paces ahead, then, I ought to find a shaft giving on

to a lower level where the water pursued its thousand-year labour of excavation. Sure enough, I came to a perpendicular drop, at which the trench stopped abruptly. I swung the lamp in the emptiness. The noise of the water now came distinctly from the shaft, which I hoped shortly to descend. For the moment, however, I climbed the side of the trench to explore the upper level, which continued on either side of the hollow brook-bed I had been walking in.

The gallery of the bats ended in an oval chamber with a horizontal ceiling, from which hung a cluster of helictites. These are stalactites which have not the usual dagger shape, but unexpected and complicated forms whose origin is still a puzzle. They are discussed at length on page 149.

Crossing this chamber, I started through a large corridor hollowed out like the previous one. The clay bed was so thick that I decided it must have come quite as much from corrosion of the rock (decalcification) as from outside.

Another sound of water came to my ears. This time it was not below, but on my level. I recognized the unsteady splash of a cascade on bare rock. I hurried on to a place where two galleries intersected. One of them, a steep one, carried a swift brook, which vanished through a crack at my feet into the depths of the cavern. I went up the brook, climbing a series of steps made by rock strata, and soon found the cascade falling noisily from the ceiling, splashing the polished boulders for yards around.

Although I held out my lamp at arm's length, I could not get a good look at the point where the water came through the ceiling. The day had already been a full one, and I was tired, so I sat down contentedly to take some notes, straighten out my ideas, and dream as I sometimes do when alone below ground.

I sat there pondering, with my eyes fixed on the flashing column of water as it splashed into the basin it had dug. All at once I recognized something I had been seeking in vain for ten years. In the centre of the basin were a multitude of splendid 'cave pearls'. Before I plunged under the cascade to gather them up, I enjoyed the sensation which every collector feels when at last he finds the ultimate rarity he has looked for.

Cave pearls are so little known that one professor of geology first heard about them from me, and so rare that I had never seen any; and here they were before my eyes! I thought of Ali Baba in the Forty Thieves' cave. It was a poor treasure judged by the market value, no doubt, but a priceless find for one who had studied every variety of concretion, and who found here in actual course of formation the strangest of them all – the oolite. I shall explain their formation at some length on page 148.

Ignoring the cold shower-bath, I filled my hat with the best pearls, some of them as large as a pigeon's egg; the smallest, pin-head size, covered the bottom of the basin, and I put a fistful in my pocket. I went away happy in my find, but not without gnawings of conscience at having pillaged the secret laboratory whose work, perhaps of centuries, had produced my booty.

The day was too far gone for me to explore the lower levels. Besides, the carbide in my lamp was running low, and I had to beat a retreat.

It may well be imagined that I came back to the cavern more than once. I explored it all the way down to the 'live' tunnels, and traced their curious course: several tributaries swelled a long subterranean stream, which I followed from end to end. Sometimes I had to crawl in the water under low ceilings. It began in an impenetrable jumble of boulders, and ended at a siphon which defied my efforts to get through.

I was surprised to find that the well so close to the outside funnel apparently had no communication with the cavern I had just explored. I therefore determined to explore the well in its turn.

It will be remembered that my rope was a few yards short of reaching a rubbish-covered platform. Here I landed at my second attempt. It was the bottom of the vertical shaft, cut from top to bottom by the straight rope line which bound me to the patch of sky overhead. A gloomy vault dug in the wall ahead of me swallowed the rubble slope I stood on. I had come down the equivalent of five storeys with my bag on my back, equipped for a difficult expedition.

As I readjusted my harness a pestilential smell greeted me. My light showed the slope cluttered with branches and jammed with carcasses in varying stages of decay. I fought down my disgust, and started firmly for the vaulted entrance, where a swarm of flies swirled busily.

Within the opening a hideous sight met my eyes: a crumbling stream of carcasses, entangled several deep, was working its way underground. Amid tangled rings of ribs were cattle skulls with menacing horns, and the open-jawed grin of horses and donkeys, once very numerous in this mountain section. A blackish, unspeakable layer at the foot of the slope moved in a venomous trickle down a vast chamber, where I was glad to find solid ground again.

The chamber was grooved down the middle by an old brook-bed of some size, which had once drained the water swallowed by the entrance shaft. Now it was empty but for the pestilent liquid thread from the carcasses. I could not take in the whole hall at one glance, so I decided to make a complete circuit, following the walls. This would give me an idea of both size and shape.

I found several tunnels opening into it. The chamber had evidently been a focal point for the streams from the various conduits. I crawled up each tunnel until it ended in an impassable crack or a small rock chimney. They all sloped steeply at the upper end, which showed that the water which once filled them had come from the surface. Some of the water still dripped slowly.

Only one tunnel declined gently; it was the outlet of the main brook-bed, and the floor of the chamber itself sloped in that direction. This, then, would be my route when I came to follow the path of the water. First I wanted to cover the interior of the chamber: so far I had merely followed its circumference.

Many a cathedral nave is smaller and lower-ceilinged than this underground dome. My reconnoitre brought me back toward the shambles at the entrance. In the faint daylight I noticed a basin such as foxes often hollow out for their litters. But foxes have a strong instinct of cleanliness, while this nest was filled with white lumps, regular coprolites, some of them quite recent. Suddenly I realized the horrible truth. A living dog had been thrown down the shaft; its fall had been broken by the branches, and the animal had lived for some time on carcasses and the puddles of water in the hall. It had dug or used the hollow, and had vegetated there despite its injuries. I was sick at heart to think of the creature's endless agony, of its howling for days, perhaps weeks, before going mad and dying. I looked around instinctively for some beseeching or threatening shadow, but there was nothing; the martyr dog must be dead along with all the rest in that charnel-house.

The low, straight tunnel leading out of the big chamber was a fine example of stratification emphasized by water. The water had gone through under pressure after accumulating in the reservoir chamber above. The pressure, amounting to several atmospheres, had left clear marks in the corridor. At the intersection of two fissures the tunnel turned at right angles; 160 feet further on it opened into an enormous chamber, the biggest I had ever seen below ground. A football field would go in easily, and the cathedral of Notre-Dame, 422 feet long, with its thirty-seven chapels, would not fill the hall.

The hall was cut up with deep ravines, studded with steep clay hillocks – a regular mountain range in miniature. In the imperfect lamplight I was tempted to think it must be a good five-eighths of a mile across, for I could neither tell how far I had gone, see where I was, nor catch sight of the ceiling. I carefully explored some ravines whose brooks cascaded into one another. I straddled along sharp clay ridges, and finally reached the end of the cavern, where the brook ran into a flat crack eight or nine inches high. Here, of course, I had to stop.

The grotto goes on, and there are probably other chambers, but a layer of clay has piled up so thick that only the water can pass. Not far from the outlet of the water (seeking a lower level as it always does) I saw a high, steep slope. I started to climb it. On my way up I saw the opening of a tunnel. I soon found it was a cul-de-sac, but as I came towards the end I found a vertical shaft in the floor.

Without a rope there was no exploring it; I could only drop stones and chunks of earth, and try to guess its depth. A few yards down my missiles bounced off a clay slope; after a short silence there was a revealing 'plop.' This showed that there was a deep basin or stream below, which I immediately dreamed of exploring. Perhaps it would bring me to the continuation of the cavern. But that day I had not the equipment for the dangerous descent.

I had already been several hours below ground, stopping constantly to take compass readings for my sketch plan of the cavern. I also had to examine alluvial deposits, erosion and corrosion phenomena, and all the thousand traces that make a new cavern fascinating.

My last task was to attack a great mound, which must have corresponded to some chimney in the ceiling. The chimney was now blocked, but for a long time it must have filled the cavern with material from outside, piling up the cone I climbed with such difficulty. The slope was steep, slippery clay and shifting sand, made still more unstable by infiltrations.

I scrambled on all fours up about a hundred feet to the top of the heap. A sad discovery awaited me. A poor dog lay there, caked in mud, its twisted tongue hanging from stiff jaws. The body was incredibly emaciated. I bent over the carcass, dead but a few days, and found one broken leg and a frightful skull wound. The wound had suppurated, and one eye was gone.

How long had the agony lasted? The vitality of dogs led one to fear it might have been weeks. Exhausted with waiting for a release that never came, the dog had conquered the fear of the dark common to most animals, and had searched deeper and deeper underground for a way out. Its mud-caked hair testified to countless falls. Finally, death had intervened.

A few days sooner, and I should have met this living spectre. Some of my fellow spelaeologists had been obliged to shoot poor, starved, mad dogs. In one chasm É.-A. Martel found an injured dog which actually had a film over its eyes from its long stay in the dark.

I returned to daylight after six hours underground, and flung myself, muddy and exhausted, on the grass. I had found one of the largest and most extraordinary caverns of the Pyrenees.

Although the cavern was sinister enough, I had every intention of going back to attempt the final shaft and its watercourse. But I came away with a painful and dangerous memento. A slight scratch became infected through contact with a carcass; three days later an enormous abscess formed in the palm of my hand. I came close to losing two fingers, and my hand was stiff for several months.

Later my wife and I went back with gloves and rope ladders to the Grotte de Cagire. We made an exact, detailed plan, and were able to prove that a cool and limpid spring known throughout the neighbourhood was the deadly resurgence of the poisoned stream.

4

AN ICE WORLD BELOW GROUND:
THE GROTTE CASTERET

*

Mirabilis in altis Dominus

*

THE celebrated group of peaks called the Massif de Gavarnie is frequented by alpinists, geographers, geologists, hunters, and naturalists; one would expect it to have no surprises left. Yet it was here that I found probably the highest ice-filled cavern in the world.

We must not confuse ice caves, mere open excavations in the front of glaciers, with frozen caverns, *glacières*, or natural ice-houses – true rock caverns, filled with ice as other grottoes harbour streams.

The largest ice-filled cavern in existence, and also the largest cavern in Europe, is in the Austrian Alps, near Salzburg. It is sixteen and three-quarter miles long; the ice occupies a mile and a quarter. The cavern is called the Eisriesenwelt (world of the ice giants); its exploration required several years of dangerous work by daring specialists with elaborate equipment.

Ice-filled grottoes exist in the Alps, in the Jura, and in the Caucasus. Many mountain massifs also have 'ice wells', where the snow accumulates during the winter, and remains for part of the summer. But real frozen caverns, glaciers underground, are geological curiosities of the first order.

No frozen cavern was known in the Pyrenees before my discovery in the heart of the Monte Perdido massif (9,700 feet).

The little village of Gavarnie, perched at 4,400 feet, is the base for climbs thereabouts. From here our little family caravan started. It consisted of my mother, my brother Martial, my wife, and myself, each combining the functions of mountaineer, guide, and porter. We set out, knapsack on back and ice-pick in hand, to explore the snowy, deserted sierras of Aragon.

We had a difficult climb in very bad weather to the Brèche de Roland. There a blizzard drove us to shelter in a tiny grotto discovered in 1909 by Abbé Gaurier, the learned Pyrenean glaciologist. We had several hours' forced seclusion in the Gaurier shelter before the tempest died down.

We began to roam the frozen snow-fields and rocks of the Marboré plateau, looking for caverns. Suddenly the wind cut a hole in the clouds, and we saw a great vestibule in a cliff. A steep, frozen-snow slope lay between it and us.

With no great enthusiasm we mounted the slope, hacking steps in the hard snow. Exciting as a new cavern may be, the work of finding it is hard, tedious, and often disappointing. But this time, when we reached the vestibule, it did not turn out, as they too often do, to be a mere overhang – it admitted us to the loveliest and most fantastic cavern I had ever explored.

A snow ledge and great rubble-heap still hid the inside of the cavern, but when we had surmounted this obstacle we could not hold back a shout. At our feet was a frozen underground lake, and a river of ice came from the bowels of the mountain beyond it.

The huge chamber was bathed in a strange, slanting, bluish-green light. There were green-grey reflections on walls and ice. Mysterious noises came from within, heralding the icy wind that blew in our faces. Where the wind met the warm outside air there was a faint mist, through which the frontier ridge, with the Brèche de Roland notch, appeared dramatically framed in the cavern mouth. Beyond was the sky of France.

My brother stood on a boulder, waving his pick, shouting and gesticulating like Professor Lidenbrock in Sneffels crater (in my old favourite *Journey to the Centre of the Earth*). In fact, the whole thing was a regular Jules Verne scene, but it was in life, not literature.

The map, checked with the pocket altimeter, showed 8,770 feet of altitude. This, then, was the highest frozen cavern on earth; that of the Dachstein, in Austria, formerly supposed to be the highest, is at 7,800 feet.

It was late, and our camp for the night – the Refuge de Gaulis, at the head of the Arrasas valley – was several hours away over broken and unfamiliar country. The weather looked threatening, the fog might suddenly return to drown everything. Furthermore, we had left our huge knapsacks at the foot of the frozen snow-field, and a search of our pockets yielded only one fat candle.

We decided on an hour's preliminary exploration nevertheless, and crossed the lake without losing a moment. Under foot was a transparent, rather thin layer of ice; we could see the water underneath. From the piled rocks we crossed to an arctic shore where the ice river, arched like a shield, pushed into the lake.

Beyond, the gallery widened, and the roof rose over a sort of subterranean glacier covering 8,400 square yards (nearly an acre and three-quarters). It was one enormous mirror, just touched by slanting, eerie light from the entrance. The ice floor was so clear that we could not tell how thick it was. Ice fringes and stalactites decorated the walls and roof, and the whole scene was indescribably fantastic.

We gathered around our pale beacon (which dazzled us quite as much as it lighted our way), and marched into the depths of the cavern in close formation. On our right we saw a low vault leading to an ice hall which stretched away out of sight. The hall received a great inflow of ice from various rock chimneys. We scanned it hastily, and then pushed on.

A colder and stronger wind met us 400 feet in, and we began to hear the crystalline jingling of little icicles falling from the ceiling. We stopped for a moment at the foot of a splendid translucent column which joined floor and roof. Here the gallery contracted sharply, and its glassy surface was broken by ice-covered rocks. Progress over this jumble of stone was not the least of the cavern's glazed difficulties.

Detours and scrambling, with frequent tumbles, finally brought us to a dangerous shaft entirely lined with ice. It seemed to fill the width of the gallery, bringing us to a dead stop. Apparently we could go no farther. We dropped some icicles in, but learned little, because they were pulverized as they went down. The faint candlelight was no use at all.

Most of the ceiling was out of sight. We were awestruck at a colossal ice tower which rose from the abyss and was lost to view overhead. Our first exploration seemed at an end, but a careful search showed a narrow passage around the well.

The candle was burning down, so for safety's sake Martial and I alone attacked the passage, leaving the ladies in the dark. Being dangerously near the shaft they had to stay motionless in the bitter cold. Once past the well we found ourselves in a broken cascade. This covered a twenty-five- or thirty-foot bank with a sixty-degree slope to the top. From below we could descry nothing but a small black hole up there. The wall was doubly difficult to climb in the dark, which the guttering candle did little to dispel. Pushed by Martial, wielding my pick, and holding the candle in my teeth, I finally managed to scramble to the top.

I started to crawl up a flattened tube in the thick ice, white as porcelain; but at each attempt an air-current trumpeting through the tunnel blew out the candle. I had, therefore, to wriggle flat on my stomach by touch through this veritable seal's lair, leaving my brother clinging to his pick in the dark at the foot of the cascade.

Happily I did not have to wriggle and shiver very long in the wind-hole. Once I was through I relit the candle, and the cavern went on and on, narrow now, but lofty. I waded knee-deep in icy slush between smooth marble walls (we were in the heart of the Marboré massif, whose name comes from marble), and so arrived at the bottom of another frozen waterfall, which hung free from the walls, like a curtain. This obstacle was several yards high, and impassable without help. Retreat grew urgent, anyway, for in the wind the candle was burning down fast.

Our return to daylight was without incident, but we were inadequately dressed for our impromptu arctic expedition, and all four of us were numbed to the marrow. The sky outside was blacker and more menacing than ever. We marched and counter-marched among the lapiaz and hostile plateaux of

Millaris and Gaulis for several hours before we arrived in the dark at the foot of Monte Perdido. We spent the night at the Refuge de Gaulis.

We put in the next few days wandering among the wild canyons and gorges of Aragon, climbing the fine peaks. Our caravan planned to finish exploring the frozen grotto a month later. At the last moment my mother and brother were prevented from joining us, and so my wife and I went alone to spend the night in the open at the Brèche de Roland. We wanted an early start and a whole day to explore the cave.

We got to the Brèche an hour before twilight, and decided to climb the Pic Taillon (10,200 feet) to watch the sunset. We were thickly surrounded by clouds, which made a splendid play of light on the mountain top. In the midst of a phantasmagoria of colours and extravagant clouds we were even lucky enough to see the Spectre of the Brocken.*

We went back by moonlight to the Brèche de Roland, and tried to camp in the Gaurier shelter, but intolerable cold and damp soon drove us out. We spent the night under the open sky at an altitude of nearly 9,500 feet. We lay awake in the cold, shivering and watching the march of the constellations in the strange stillness of high altitudes.

By dawn we had already disturbed a herd of timid chamois, crossed the little river of the Brèche, surveyed the boulder-strewn desert which had kept previous alpinists away, and crossed the underground lake, which at this hour of the morning was frozen hard.

According to my calculations this second exploration was sure to bring us out on the opposite side of the mountain. The formation of the glacier could scarcely be explained except by the existence of two orifices, sending a current of cold air through the cavern, and we hoped to surmount any natural obstacles we might find.

Our first step was to explore the huge hall which we had

*The Spectre of the Brocken is an enormously magnified shadow of the person who sees it, cast on the clouds by a sinking sun in high mountains. The phenomenon is so called from having been first observed on the Brocken in the Harz Mountains in 1780.

glimpsed a month before. Its vast roof was all in one piece, spanning an ice-field with an estimated area of 3,350 square yards; its impressiveness may be imagined.

Huge blocks off the ceiling were set in the ice, which was so clear that we could see tiny pebbles frozen six or seven feet deep. Cracks in the vault furnished a considerable influx of ice to feed the lake. The largest of these streams filled a vertical cleft, and formed a translucent cascade sixty or eighty feet high. Its top was lost to sight.

The temperature of the hall never rises above the freezing-point, and it is very likely that the lower layers of ice are 'fossil', formed in the course of geologic ages and never melted.

Our light was better than at our first visit, and we were soon familiar with the terrain. We gave up our slow and cautious advance, and skated frantically across the smooth, perfect ice. This sport was probably then indulged in for the first time below ground, and it combined business with pleasure by warming us up a bit after twelve hours' intense cold.

We enjoyed ourselves like children. In the echoing vastness the sound of our sliding and tumbling and laughter became deafening. It echoed and re-echoed until we could not talk a hundred feet apart; the syllables overlapped and interfered.

We stopped for a moment to identify a bird with out-stretched wings, frozen in the ice eighteen inches below our feet. The ice was so transparent that we plainly saw the coral claws and beak of a *choucas alpin*, a common species in the cliffs around the Brèche de Roland.

Back in the main gallery we found that a month of summer had made little change in the condition of the ice cave. A few icicles had melted, and there were some stripes thawed in the mirror under foot.

Having no rope we could neither explore nor sound the ice-lined oubliette, so we cautiously passed it by. We put in some time taking flashlight photographs, drawing a sketch map by compass, and making various observations. Then we started off again across the lake, where our special hobnails were extremely helpful. A horizontal fissure head-high in the right-hand wall soon attracted my attention. First I threw in some ice splinters, which rebounded and fell with a 'plop' indicating water. A moment later I followed the ice chips, sliding head first into a sort of letter-box with my feet in the air. I braked instantly with hands, back, and knees to keep out of the water, which was so clear that I had not seen it until my hat dipped in. By frantic efforts I managed to avoid a complete bath. Ordinarily, immersion would have been a trifle, but to-day I was already numb, my boots were frozen, and in wet clothes I could not have stayed in the cavern.

I was in a narrow cleft, my legs and arms spreadeagled against the sides. The water, stirred by my struggles, flashed below me in the dim candlelight. I presume the brook had not frozen because it was sheltered from the freezing draught that sweeps down the grotto.

The channel turned at right angles a few yards ahead. I went on, candle in teeth, still bracing myself on the walls, and clinging to the slightest footholds. At a second turn the tube still continued; I could take no chances of a bath, so for once I had to turn back. I rejoined my wife, who had of course seen nothing, but had heard my scraping, splashing, and groans.

After a moment's rest we attacked the first ice cascade. We got up after some difficulty, trailing our picks and heavy knapsacks. The perpendicular upper cascade was even more ticklish. Our combined heights were not enough, but I was ready to try anything, so I ungallantly put my iron-shod feet on my wife's shoulders; I got hold of some projections in the ice, and hauled myself up. My valiant partner opportunely made a stirrup by driving a pick into a crack. With this help I reached a ledge, and thence the top of the cascade. An instant later the other half of the expedition was vigorously hoisted to my side along with knapsacks and picks.

We were in a narrow, steeply rising, ice-coated gallery; from the top came a faint ray of daylight. The climb was soon over, and we found ourselves in a rotunda-shaped chamber, its ceiling pierced with a round hole. Several yards above our heads the hole picked out a disk of dark blue sky.

We tramped round and round like bears in the pit, with

our noses in the air, until we noticed a small opening at the side, hidden from us at first by a snow-bank. Slipping in, we soon found that but a few yards of limestone separated us from the surface. The roof of the tunnel was pierced with holes like that in the rotunda.

I picked the easiest shaft to climb, and had just thrown off my knapsack for greater freedom of motion when we were dumbfounded to hear a long, skilfully modulated whistle from above. Where could we be? Was there a man at this hour of the morning in a spot we had thought absolutely deserted? He would surely be as surprised at us as we at him.

By vigorous exertions I got up the shaft, and popped from the mountain like a jack-in-the-box. The whistler did indeed show surprise, but did not budge from the rock he was perched on. Of the two I was the more surprised: instead of the Spanish smuggler or stray alpinist I had expected, I saw a graceful whistling nuthatch. For an hour it kept flitting around us from rock to rock, displaying its pink wings and giving its musical whistle. Like its fellow-inhabitant of high altitudes, the snow-finch, this rock nuthatch rarely sees human beings, and curiosity makes it tame.

Meanwhile I hoisted up my wife by a pick-handle, and we sat down to take stock of our situation.

We had entered the mountain through a cliff on the western flank of an unnamed peak about 8,985 feet high. We had come out on the eastern slope in the midst of a wild confusion which the geologists call *lapiaz* – a name which speaks volumes to anyone who has ever tried to cross such a formation. A slice of bread has fewer holes than lapiaz, with its chasms, oubliettes, trap-holes, fissures, tunnels, funnels, knife-like ridges. In such terrain one is driven to the wildest acrobatics.

We took the trouble to study about a hundred acres of the lapiaz. Erosion (the chemical action of water and snow) and alternating freezes and thaws have worn the limestone, scratched, gnawed, and tormented it into its present chaotic shape. The same process has dried up the neighbouring lake of Millaris, which hides under snow eight or nine months a year, and is an arid plain in midsummer.

This particular lapiaz has the peculiarity that all the holes communicate through a series of chambers, domes, corridors, and branches fifteen to thirty feet below ground. The labyrinth is faintly lit by the holes in the vaults. The lapiaz, in other words, has been hollowed out until it forms one long cavern. At this altitude (8,775 feet) there are frequent heavy snows, and what is now called the Pic de la Grotte is snow-capped from October to the end of June. Only in July, August, and September do its varicoloured slopes and landslides appear.

The snow which covers and chokes the lapiaz gradually melts, but a few yards below ground it lasts all summer, sheltered from sun, warm winds, and rain. This underground snow-field is an almost unique phenomenon. One wanders far through spotless chambers filled with great snow cones corresponding to the holes overhead. Melted snow and a trickle from above form treacherous pools of clear water, invisible in the white snow. Sometimes the snow touches the ceiling, blocking further progress, but there is every reason to believe that the strange cavern continues uninterrupted under the lapiaz.

The real interest is not in the lapiaz, however, but in the frozen cavern, which was hollowed out by a violent torrent during a much warmer geological epoch than the present. Now a change in climate has 'fossilized' the water-course, which works in slow motion, masses of ice taking the place of the old brawling stream.

The transformation from snow to water, and thence to ice, takes place in the steep tunnel connecting the snow banks under the lapiaz with the cavern proper. It is produced by the slope and the violent cold blast sweeping down to the underground glacier. One actually sees the change going on in the tunnel above the translucent cascade which we climbed with such difficulty on the way up.

Such, in brief, were the course and result of our exploration. We spent a total of three weeks on it, living on bread and cheese and glacier water, shivering under the stars and baking under the Spanish noonday sun. We had the satisfaction of seeing the cavern christened the Grotte Casteret in honour of our family discovery, and among other distinctions we received a personal note of congratulation from His Majesty Alfonso XIII for discovering the world's highest frozen cavern in what was then his kingdom.

The venerable É.-A. Martel thought the Grotte Casteret and the Eisriesenwelt 'full of promise' for hydrology, and I have no hesitation in saying that the extraordinary region of the Monte Perdido in the Aragonese Pyrenees still has many surprises in store for anyone who will get off the beaten track, and methodically explore this stony desert.

5

THE DEEPEST ABYSS IN FRANCE,
THE GOUFFRE MARTEL

*

Abyssus abyssum invocat
DAVID (Psalm xlii. 8)

*

IN Ariège, south of Saint-Girons at the French-Spanish border, a water-power corporation, L'Union Pyrénéenne Électrique, has spent several years developing the power from the streams in a mountain cirque, or amphitheatre, the Cirque du Lez. Here rises the stream of that name, a confluent of the Salat.

It is a bold undertaking going quietly and persistently forward here – the diversion into one conduit of all the waters of the Cirque du Lez. This conduit will carry the water to a neighbouring cirque, where it will form a reservoir of 3,712,500,000 gallons. The water will fall 3,400 feet from the reservoir to the turbines of an electric power plant developing 40,000 horse-power, now under construction in the valley. Altogether this development, which I have sketched too briefly, will be one of the boldest and most remarkable French power projects.

In the course of a preliminary hydraulic survey, one of the company engineers, M. Paul Catala, discovered that two small lakes high up in the cirque had a mysterious underground outlet. To learn where the water reappeared was essential, for it seemed likely to escape the diversion.

The usual experiment of colouring the water confirmed this fear. A pound of fluorescein was thrown into the torrent of Albe at its disappearance. Eighteen hours later the colour appeared in another torrent in the vast amphitheatre, that of the Cigalère. The colour was found to have come out through a peculiar resurgence in the very bed of the second torrent, revealing an extraordinary and improbable-seeming underground passage. The resurgence was 650 feet below the projected conduit, which was to drain the cirque at an altitude of 6,715 feet.

It now seemed difficult, if not impossible, to divert the torrent of Albe. Either the water had to be pumped up 650 feet from the resurgence to the conduit, or the swallowing of the water at a similar distance above the tunnel must be prevented. Ordinarily it would have been easy to transport the water along the surface to the point where it was needed; but here this was impossible because of the limestone, which is so full of faults as to be a regular sieve. In that part of the amphitheatre it absorbs all surface water.

After exhausting the usual means of controlling the Albe torrent, the Union Pyrénéenne Électrique submitted their problem to me. It was the more difficult because both disappearance and resurgence were impassable. The conditions were most discouraging, and I took them as a personal challenge.

The region to be studied, straddling the French-Spanish border ridge, is a living example of the familiar comparison between the two slopes of the Pyrenees. On the north is the steep Lez amphitheatre. Its walls are abrupt and covered with frozen snow; cliffs striped with waterfalls drop from 5,500 feet to the forest zone, and so to the bottom of the valley, where the torrent of Lez unites all the streams of the cirque.

On the south is the Spanish mining district of Liat. Its high plateau pastures have uncertain little valleys studded with lakes and ponds, and they join a knot of arid mountains whose nondescript shapes go on and on as far as the great Val d'Aran.

The geological principles by which one tries to predict underground waters' paths are difficult to apply here; the structure of the region is very complex. I always try, therefore, to trace underground waters by direct exploration. With that intention I went to the amphitheatre of Lez.

My first step was to go and look at the resurgence where the fluorescein had come up. I took leave of the engineers, and started up the valley where the plant was being built. My path was a mule track which had served for two centuries in working the Sentein iron and zinc mines, located in the cirque at an altitude of 6,500 feet, and now abandoned, though not exhausted.

I climbed through the woods for two hours, and then came out into the pastures, peopled with grazing sheep. I made a flanking march, crossing a number of iron-bearing brooks, and so hurried toward the resurgence in the gorge of the Cigalère torrent.

I hoped the resurgence might not be so impenetrable as it had looked; perhaps I could wriggle through a crack that seemed too small to people unaccustomed to the difficulties of caverns. Alas! When I reached the little torrent, at the foot of a 325-foot cliff, I had to bow to the facts. Not only was the resurgence impenetrable, but the whole stream went entirely out of sight under an enormous heap of debris which blocked the ravine for a hundred-odd yards.

Below the heap the water reappeared, springing up imperceptibly through jumbled stones. I found the outflow higher than the water above the landslip. The resurgence was here, sure enough; but seldom has an underground stream come to light in more unpromising fashion. In my disgust I saw nothing better to do than to take the water temperature above and below the wretched landslide. The thermometer showed a drop of two degrees centigrade between the two points – more proof of a new stream's arrival.

Then I stuck my pick in the ground, dropped my knapsack on the grass, and sat down to look at the splendid cliff which towered above me. My eye followed a flock of noisy jackdaws whirling and perching on airy ledges too small to see, and suddenly I noticed a black hole in the wall. I had seen it from afar, and had taken it for one of the many mine tunnels of the neighbourhood. Now I saw that the yawning hole was too big and irregular for man's handiwork. It must be a grotto, or at least a natural porch. I climbed for it at once: I can never leave the slightest cavern uninspected.

As I hurried up the steep, crumbling slopes which guard it,

I thought of unnumbered disappointments, and of the great proportion of false grottoes and insignificant hollows in cliffs. But I also recalled some lucky finds, particularly the frozen cavern in the Marboré, where I had climbed six years before as I was climbing now, hacking steps in the frozen snow.

I reached the opening, and went in. I was in a roughly horizontal corridor twelve or fifteen feet wide and ten or twelve feet high. It shrank quickly, and a rocky barrier and semi-darkness cut off the view. The ground was cluttered with broken stone; not a breath of air, not a sound from within, nothing indicated a cavern of any consequence.

At the rock barrier I stopped a moment to light a candle, a package of which I always have in my bag. My eyes were not yet accustomed to the darkness, and I went ahead almost by touch. The gallery turned downward; I walked cautiously on a soft floor cumbered with wet and slippery blocks.

Suddenly I was rooted to the spot; I heard the familiar sound of distant running water. In an instant I knew I had providentially discovered the torrent I was looking for. I hurried towards it, slipping and stumbling down the sloping tunnel. Excited and impatient as I was, I had to be careful; the candlelight was bad, and the slope grew steeper and steeper.

The noise of the water became louder and clearer. I heard the stream a few yards off, and then I saw it, whirling over its gravel bed and rushing with vile sucking noises into a fissure. I was a hundred yards and more from daylight, and forty feet below the entrance. The entrance had evidently been an old overflow, a dead resurgence of the underground torrent. Where I stood, the water entered an impenetrable crack, and following an invariable hydrologic law it would return to daylight at the obstructed resurgence in the ravine of the Cigalère. This end was a cul-de-sac, but upstream I saw a spacious gallery, where the stream ran between earth banks. I started in that direction.

Here the banks rose into a steep gully, and I climbed all the way out over them, because it was very ticklish work clinging to the slippery slope. The preservation of the light, after all, was vital, and a tumble into the water would have been perilous. Once out of the gully, I found the floor broken and rugged.

I was thunderstruck at the sudden vastness of the cavern. My dancing candle-flame showed confused hillocks of earth, and then a pitch-black void. I hurled stones as far and as high as I could, but I heard them fall without hitting walls or ceiling.

The size of the cavern made me uneasy. No solitude is comparable to the bowels of the earth, no night so dark as the blackness underground. I was walking in a nightmare; it seemed that I had to wrestle with impenetrable nothingness. I would gladly spend days alone underground – but only when I know the topography, and can keep in touch with something palpable, such as a wall.

Here I had nothing, and each step took me further into a void from which I might never return. I faced about, and made instinctively for the stream. Once I found it, I followed its winding course like Ariadne with her thread.

I passed an enormous stone obelisk with its base in the water. Other boulders rose out of the darkness, and soon I reached a great rock barrier with water cascading out. Was this the source of the stream?

And was this huge heap of rocks the remnant of a cave-in that had blocked the cavern? The idea occurred to me as I scaled the pile. Even when I stood on the topmost boulder my light did not reach the ceiling, however, and I went down the other side of the stone mountain, and found the stream running free at the bottom. Now I could be assured of going far below ground.

I went on and on upstream. Finally I came in sight of one wall, and then of the other. They closed in to form a corridor with the brook in the middle. Little by little it became an ordinary underground river; I even caught sight of the ceiling now and then. I had recovered my nerve after a scary start, and was not at all surprised to find the gallery narrowing at a turn until its whole width was filled with smooth water. There was no longer any worry about getting lost. Of course it was uncomfortable to walk in the icy water, but that was part of the day's work underground, and I did not hesitate.

I waded a long way, with interruptions to scale boulders or wriggle through tight spots. After travelling what I took to be about five-eighths of a mile (my estimate later proved correct) I reached a point where the roof of the cavern sank until it touched the water. It was a siphon.

My usual method of attack in such cases, by diving, was useless here, because the bed of the stream was so choked with sand that I could not even crawl in.

I had to turn back. But twenty yards from the end I saw a raised tunnel which seemed to be the continuation of the cavern. I was so tired and nervous, and my light was so poor, that I decided to go back, and put off the rest of the exploration to another day. I reached the open air without incident, though the cold water did nothing to help matters. That very evening I was able to announce my discovery, and get up a second expedition.

A group consisting of the engineering director, M. Catala, four young engineers, and myself attacked the cavern again the following day. With our strong acetylene lamps we learned that the hall in which I had nearly got lost was one of the most enormous ever discovered. We crossed it, climbed the great barrier, and started wading upstream.

The solitude and mystery of yesterday had given way to high spirits; the men were gay and excited over the new sport. Where I had dared the black silence in fear and trembling, we splashed and shouted noisily, and the lamps sparkled in the water. The spell of the cavern was broken; the dangers, insuperable to a lone man, were now as nothing.

We arrived in high spirits at the siphon, which each man insisted on seeing for himself. Then we back-tracked as far as a rivulet above the raised gallery which I had seen the day before. Here we stopped to rest and take counsel, while the more delicate members of the party emptied their shoes and wrung out their clothes.

I took occasion to point out that the worn-out shoes I use below ground have the advantage (being full of holes) of not holding water. My system led to an excited discussion, of the

kind always heard among alpinists and hunters, on the subject
of shoes and equipment. The wet clothes were hampering and
chilling, and every one agreed that I was right in exploring
half-naked. This custom has many advantages which can be
appreciated only on trial.

More or less dry, and more or less convinced, we decided
to go on by the narrow tunnel. We crawled in one by one. For
a moment the bottle-neck, the key to all our hopes, seemed to
contract. We had to twist and wriggle to accommodate ourselves to an irregular passage.

Suddenly those behind, still struggling in the tube, heard
exclamations of delight from the front. The vanguard had
just come out into a wider corridor, entirely lined with snow-
white deposit. Explorers' fever took hold of us all. We all
wanted to lead the procession; the scramble threatened the
fragile stalactites. Silvery tinkles showed that we broke some
off in passing. The destruction was unintended and largely
unavoidable; but still the immaculate beauty of the walls
made us slow up, lest we profane a temple worthy of the
Thousand and One Nights.

The cavern shrank again, the walls almost touched, and
the ceiling seemed to join the floor. The remaining passage
was a regular cat-hole, and we had to wriggle in in true cat
fashion. We bowed one another in as if in a drawing-room;
M. Catala was the first to go through, flat on his stomach. He
crawled laboriously, while the rest of us waited anxiously with
our heads together and our lamps on the ground. His feet
disappeared; we heard the rubbing of cloth, the grating of
hobnails on the stone, a stifled groan. Finally there was a
moment's silence while he stood up and pointed his light
ahead. The next sign of life was a roar of astonished triumph;
finally we heard him shout through the tunnel: 'The white
sea!'

His words recalled one of the most extraordinary scenes in
my old favourite, Verne's *Journey to the Centre of the Earth*. I
flung myself into the tunnel, and scrambled out at the other
end, followed by the rest of the party.

A white, brilliant, coagulated surface spread out under our

feet; it was terminated by high cliffs, also white. Nowhere but underground could we have seen such a spectacle. This smooth, unbroken expanse was neither water nor ice; it was a floor of moist, shiny stalagmite. The walls were covered with a dull, granular deposit, deceptively like the sides of an ice-floe.

The frozen sea rang under our feet as we walked. The whole thing was so like a polar scene that we thought we felt a chill breeze. So we did, in fact; it was not an illusion. The resemblance was unimaginably perfect. We walked Indian file through an arctic wilderness, and the unreal, diffuse light of our lamps must have been like that of the midnight sun. To cap it all, the stalagmite cracked and gave under my weight, and my leg sank in as I jumped away. I returned cautiously to the gaping hole; it was full of clear water, of the turquoise cast peculiar to glaciers.

If I had been alone when I saw these marvels, I would hardly dare describe them now for fear of sceptical smiles. But the absolute stupefaction of my companions is a sign that I am not exaggerating. And there were yet more astonishing things to come.

The white sea narrowed to a winding fjord between beetling cliffs; then the surface rose to the foot of a petrified waterfall. Beyond, the gallery continued narrow; its walls were covered with a spiny deposit which hooked and scratched the would-be passer-by. We scrambled up an abrupt rise out of the corridor into a spacious chamber.

Here we stood speechless. Just when we thought we had exhausted our powers of admiration, we stepped into a fairy palace. Hundreds of caverns and countless strange stories and pictures had not prepared me for marvels like these.

Stalactites and crystals sparkled everywhere; their profusion, their whiteness, their shapes were fantastic beyond belief. We were inside a precious stone; it was a palace of crystal. But that is a mere cliché for what we saw. I will not pile up superlatives by attempting a general description. Even in colouring and delicacy the formations surpassed the most gorgeous flowers of nature.

There were microscopic stalactites and flawlessly transparent giant crystals. There were shiny formations, dull formations, smooth formations, spiny formations, milky, red, black, crude green formations. The colours came from mineral infiltrations, of which the mountain has a rich and varied store. Finally, there were two entirely new phenomena, still unexplained: huge needles as fine as cobwebs, which trembled and broke at a breath, and silver strings with the brilliance of silk yarn, which dangled from roof and walls. These extraordinary mineral cords could be wound around one's finger, and even tied in knots. M. Alfred Lacroix, the eminent mineralogist of the Academy of Sciences, tells me that they are extraordinary forms of gypsum.

Amid all these wonders we advanced but slowly. We could not avoid trampling on flowers, crushing masses of crystal with our hobnailed boots, breaking glass rods and swords and coral-bushes. We went several hundred yards through chambers and vestibules. Constant new splendours kept us breathless. The least of them would have been the crown jewel of any cavern open to visitors.

There was a fork, and I led the way up the left-hand tunnel. It narrowed quickly: we had to stoop, keeping an eye out for the sharp stalactites which threatened us, actually wounding one of the party. As I was studying the ceiling, with its countless sparkling swords of Damocles, I suddenly seemed to be knee-deep in bushes. It was indeed a bush, but a bush of crystal – the loveliest and most delicate in the cavern. Immediately afterwards, as if the grotto had used up every possible formation, all display suddenly stopped. We walked bent double, in an absolutely bare rock tube which grew shallower and shallower. Soon we had to walk on our knees, then on all fours; at last we had to crawl. We were in a regular burrow, which rose, plunged, and rose again. Such undulations are quite common, and are produced by successive accumulations of sand left by dead streams.

At the end of a particularly steep plunge, down which I coasted with a swimming motion, I came out in a chamber at the intersection of several shallow tunnels. We made fruitless attempts to negotiate tubes too small for us, and then gathered for a moment in the chamber. Finally I saw a very low and unpromising opening which we had overlooked. I crawled in. Meanwhile my companions, thinking they had reached the end of the cavern, set to building a cairn in the middle of the chamber to mark the furthest point of the expedition.

I dragged along, flat on my stomach, between floor and roof. My cheek was pressed to the ground, and I flattened out my feet as much as I could. With great difficulty I gained a few yards, but then was absolutely unable to get further. I did stretch out my arm ahead, and found I could poke the lamp through on its side. In this position I tried to look ahead.

Behind I heard the voices of the men and the noise of their cairn-building, all damped and confused by the low tunnel. Ahead, I was excited to see the lantern flicker in a cold air-current which blew in my face, proving that the cavern went on. Unfortunately there was no getting through; it would have been necessary to dig a passage in the rock. There was nothing for it but to turn back, and announce that we had reached the end of the practicable cavern.

My companions were not a bit disappointed. Several of them had never been in a cave before, and were still thunderstruck at what they had seen. They thought it remarkable that we had got so far.

We all guessed how much ground we had covered. The estimates were varied, but all were enormously exaggerated. When I guessed that we had made about a mile, there was a chorus of surprise and protest; but I stuck to my figure, and it later turned out to be right.

We put in the cairn a leaf from a note-book with the date and the names of the explorers: Brouca, Casteret, Catala, Danglas, Dubreuil. Then we decided that the new cavern should bear the name of the beautiful cliff from which it opens. A mile from daylight we gave three resounding cheers for the Grotte de la Cigalère.

I had every intention of trying again a few days later, but rain and the first snows of October swelled the stream, and shut off the cavern for many months.

Madame Casteret visits a Bat Colony

The Resurgence in the Pyrenees

The Diversion Tunnel

Into the Abyss

Stalactites and Stalagmites

A Subterranean Lake

Casteret in his Pneumatic Canoe

An Underground River

Gypsum Flowers

The Rock Barrier after the Fall

Mont Néthou in the Trou du Tora Region

Trou du Tora

The Western Garonne

During the long winter evenings my thoughts often turned to the great cavern. In imagination I saw its rushing torrent, the flashing stalactites plunged again in gloom after our furtive passage, all the useless splendour seen but once in centuries of centuries. And often, indeed, I dreamed of the final crack, where the icy wind blew from the depths I was burning to explore. No cavern had ever taken such a hold on my imagination.

Finally, the following August, I attacked again. This time the conditions were excellent; the stream was passable, and I had the oldest and best of partners, my brother Martial. I was careful also not to forget my pick, on which all my hopes were built.

We went straight through to the stopping-place of the year before, and squirmed into the flat tube at the end. I went to work with a will. The rock ceiling was impregnable, but the floor consisted of an inch-and-a-half stalagmite crust over sand. It was not an easy job to use the pick as I lay flat on my stomach, with no room to swing, but gradually I chipped away a little channel in the floor. We had to wriggle along it like snakes.

The further I went, the stronger grew the blast of air. Despite our vigorous exercise we found the walls and the wind uncomfortably icy. My brother lay shivering behind me at full length, and he had to crawl back to the little chamber so that he could move around and get warm. The wind kept putting out the acetylene lamp. I tried to shelter the flame with a stalagmite slab, but it did not work, and I had to do my mole's task by my electric flash-light.

I worked desperately for an hour, and then the battery began to give out. But I had gained sixty or seventy feet, and I could see the ceiling rising beyond. With my last strength I squirmed frantically, scraping myself as I forced my way through, and thus burst into a passage where I could stand up. My brother followed close at my heels.

We had walked but ten yards when the corridor came to a sudden end. But an air-hole close to the ground emitted a fierce blast. It was the most violent wind-hole I have ever seen. A handkerchief spread in front of it cracked like a flag, and grains of sand from somewhere whipped our faces; the lamps were blown out instantly. Blocks of stone wedged into the hole barred our passage; we would have to come back with crowbars.

Difficulties and disappointments are so much the rule underground that persistence is at a premium; in a book these repeated attempts easily become tedious. With this excuse I will ask the reader to follow me on a fourth trip into the cavern.

This time I had the company of two engineers, Messrs Catala and Vuillemin, and two miners, who soon opened up the wind-hole with crowbars. Luckily it was not a long conduit, but simply a hole opening into the roof of a huge hall. At the bottom, forty feet below, was the underground stream again. We went down an earth pitch to the brook, which we tried to follow on narrow overhanging ledges. Suddenly one of these cornices gave way under me, and I fell in. This gave me one advantage over my companions: I had no further need to keep dry. In any case it soon became impossible to go on without taking to the water, so I stuck to my bath, and set out, leaving the rest of the crowd perched on the ledges.

With one hand I clung to the bank to keep my footing; with the other I held the lamp at arm's length. I went at top speed, for the cold was unbearable. This lasted for a hundred yards; the river ran in a narrow but very deep cleft, where I bumped into a pile of boulders rising from the water. Beyond the barrier I heard the impressive grumbling of a waterfall. I wriggled apprehensively under the huge stones, and managed to come out safe on the other side. My lamp took on a halo from the heavy mist that whipped the dripping boulders. In a few strides I reached the middle of a pool below a waterfall, which fell noisily from a height of thirty feet.

The wall from which it fell was absolutely smooth and perpendicular, and the water came down in sheets, quite away from the walls. The obstacle was insuperable.

There was nothing for it but to beat a retreat. Still, the day had been a success beyond our dreams, for we had found the torrent again, and made several hundred yards. I shivered in my wet clothes all the way back, but before we were out of the cavern I had formed a new plan of attack.

Several days later I went back with two men of proved energy and devotion. We had with us five pieces of two-and-a-quarter-inch iron pipe, each six feet six inches long. These could be screwed end to end, forming a rod strong enough for me to try scaling the thirty-foot waterfall.

The pipes were heavy and clumsy enough anyway, and moving them was doubly hard because of the precautions necessary to prevent battering the threads. Our struggles in getting them through the water, the rock-piles, and the low tunnels may be imagined.

Finally we did reach the foot of the waterfall. Joining the pipes by hand was very hard work; some of the threads had been injured, and we had to work in the water. Then we raised the thirty-two-and-a-half-foot column against the cliff – a feat of strength accomplished not without alarming bumps and much trembling for the joints. All three of us were well soaked by the time we had stood the long rod upright in the axis of the waterfall. Its upper end rose clear of the fall, and neatly reached the ledge.

We stepped back out of the way of the waterfall to catch our breath. My companions turned to me, but I cut a sorry figure, for my hands were numb, and I was in no shape for the strenuous climb. It took me some minutes to regain the use of my fingers. Finally I put on a sou'wester with chin-strap, hung the unlit lantern from my belt, and took the lamp, lit, in my teeth. I walked with lowered head into the waterspout, blindly seized the pipe with both hands, and swarmed with all my might up this new form of greasy pole. The icy downpour soaked me through in a twinkling, and hammered savagely at my back and shoulders. I could not even climb so fast as I would have liked, because I had to keep an eye on the balance of the pipe, which threatened to slide off. The further I climbed, the less violent the waterfall, but the more flexible the pipe. I had but one thought – to climb up where I could breathe.

Suddenly my hands hit the upper edge of the cliff, and my head popped out of the water. This was the crucial moment, for I had to hoist myself, get my balance, and let go of the pipe. I managed all right, and found myself clinging to a boulder in the midst of the torrent. I relighted the acetylene lamp, and glanced at my companions, pointing their lamps at me from the water thirty feet below. We had agreed that I should reconnoitre alone once I got up. The current in the narrow gorge ahead of me was so strong that I could not wade against it. Climbing on ledges, I reached a sort of hanging balcony; I got above the rapids by the air line, and took to the calm water again.

There were two new cascades, which I scaled by using the rugged surrounding walls.

Five hundred feet upstream from my companions I was stopped by a deep basin. The only way round it was on a doubtful-looking ledge. The temperature of the water that day was thirty-seven degrees Fahrenheit, and a new bath was anything but tempting; I was frozen and worn out. After five hours' struggling in the water my hands were rigid. I was sure to be stopped sooner or later by some new waterfall anyway. Finally, how would my water-tight box of matches behave in case of need, and how could I strike them with only senseless hooks on the ends of my arms? The cold water and the accumulated difficulties were too much for me. I had to turn back.

I did not get another chance at the cascades until the following year. In the meantime I had an assignment in the caves of the Moroccan Atlas.

I must not tarry long over the next expedition, though it was both exciting and instructive. My wife, who had been unable to take part in the preceding campaigns, was now of the party. With her help I did good work despite unfavourable conditions. The cascades, swelled by recent snowfall, were both violent and glacial. At one of them, where the footholds were rotten schist, my wife fell over backward into a deep, boiling pool, and had to swim hard to regain the bank.

Further up we had the satisfaction of discovering a curious underground tributary whose existence I had predicted.

Finally I went on alone. It was my turn to swim a pool at thirty-seven degrees Fahrenheit, and then I reached the foot of a seventh high, vertical cascade, defended by a deep pond. The obstacle was insuperable. Although the cavern goes further, it ceases at this point to be negotiable.

The last expedition took ten hours, and we were frightfully exhausted; but I did not mind, for the solution of the problem was in sight, and we had passed the mile-and-a-quarter limit of length rarely exceeded by French caverns.

The water was really too cold, and when I scaled the series of dangerous cascades the difficulties piled up too much for a lone man. I therefore gave up the Cigalère cavern, and decided to see what I could find higher up, near the disappearance of the torrent of the Albe. I was already familiar with the disappearance of the torrent. At an altitude of 3,040 feet it suddenly drops through the crevices of a rocky defile. I began systematically covering that section. It is a desert where carpets of rhododendron partly hide twisted rocky banks and ledges full of cracks, funnels, and clefts – regular lapiaz.

I hoped that these signs of underground watercourses might lead me to a system of caverns where I could get in to look for the lost torrent. I spent several days vainly scouring the terrain, finding a quantity of funnels, all blocked a few yards down.

One day I was making the rounds of a series of these funnels. Happening to look down one smaller than the rest, I saw a black hole big enough to let a man in, with a thin mist rising from it to show its great depth. Against just such a discovery I had brought along my outfit for preliminary work. I let down into the hole a thin, strong rope, sixty-five feet long, first making the upper end fast to a rocky projection. I slid through the narrow opening of the chasm, and stopped thirty feet down on a stone chunk caught in the narrow well. Thus far the shaft had had the shape and dimensions of a chimney, and descending it was a matter of scraping hard against the sides. Below the rock the chimney was considerably larger. I swung the rope in all directions without hitting anything.

Now for a simple trick of my trade. I unfolded a newspaper, set fire to it, and dropped it into the blackness. The paper spiralled slowly down, lighting a bell-shaped chamber. It came to rest, and burned out near the end of the rope, which dangled a yard from the floor.

I slid down to bottom sixty-five feet below ground. Then I stood motionless, listening. Underground the sense of hearing is almost one's chief reliance. Nothing could have pleased and excited me more just then than the mournful plaint which rose to my ears. There was a sighing and wailing, amplified by echoes, distorted by the strange acoustics of caverns – the voice of the Albe torrent.

Another burning newspaper brushed down an almost vertical shaft, and stopped thirty feet below me. I descended with the candle in my teeth, clinging to projections of the rock instead of using a rope. At the end of this third stage, nearly a hundred feet below ground, I set foot on a pile of boulders. Under them I heard the stream, and in spots saw it hastening ever deeper into the bowels of the mountain. My candle dimly showed me a vast sloping gallery filled with boulders, a regular ante-room of hell. I worked my way cautiously downward. I was delighted to have got so far, and at the same time fearful of being lost alone in an unknown abyss. Embracing the rocks as I slid, I reached a point where the torrent vanished through a sluice under a heap of enormous blocks that almost touched the slanting roof. It was certainly not impossible to scale the pile, but careful scrutiny showed me that the blocks were precariously balanced, and the least weight might upset tons of boulders.

Nevertheless that was the spot I returned to a few days later, this time using a rope ladder. I had with me the two assistants – now officially so + who had helped me with the iron pipes in the lower cavern. These two, Cabalet and Lledo, were a pair as unlike as possible in looks and disposition, but alike in a courage and devotion which they soon had occasion to show.

We stood in a row at the foot of the boulders while I studied the menacing structure. The presence of companions did not diminish the danger, of course, but still I felt more courageous. Fumbling cautiously and respectfully, I ventured over the gigantic mantrap. Agility and lightness of foot were my sole reliance as I climbed to the top and down on the other side, but nothing stirred. I was delighted at my luck, and hardly less so to find the torrent still hurrying down the steep corridor. My companions, emboldened, if not reassured, passed in their turn.

In quick succession we went down two cascades twelve or fifteen feet high, to find ourselves stopped on the brink of a third. Our burning paper showed us that this one fell a hundred feet in two cascades. My only rope ladder remained at the mouth of the shaft, linking us to the outside world. We had only a rope with us. I slid down it, supported from above by Cabalet and Lledo, who exerted themselves to keep me out of the centre of the waterfall and spare me a rough and icy ducking. The further down I went, the more the water spread, and I got my shower-bath anyway.

At the bottom of the precipice I let go the rope, and followed the leaping torrent over heaps of rocks down the great sloping tunnel. The gallery was long and steep, and I was like an ant in the underground maze. I had to skirt huge blocks fallen from the ceiling; some of them must have been forty or fifty cubic yards in volume. The further I went, the larger grew the cavern, and the steeper the slope. My progress was a disorderly scramble down Titan pitches where the water splashed and foamed. I began to lose all sense of time, distance, and depth. Still I descended; I was determined to go on until some insuperable obstacle put a stop to my exploration.

Finally, five hundred feet below ground, I halted on the brink of a perpendicular precipice over which the cataract fell with a deafening roar. My burning sheets of paper were instantly snatched and drowned in the waterspout. I rolled down boulders which disappeared without a distinguishable sound or an echo to tell me the depth of the abyss. For a long time I stood dreaming and dazed before the cararact. I forgot what I was there for, forgot my companions anxiously waiting above. I was leaning alone over the mouth of hell.

At that time my outfit consisted of but a hundred feet of rope ladder and some ropes. But some days later, by acrobatic feats, my faithful porters and I managed to carry to the brink of the last abyss a 325-foot rope belonging to the power company.

Leaving early in the morning, we had climbed under crushing loads from the works to the mouth of the funnel (altitude 9,225 feet). Then the painful descent of 500 feet, with repeated wettings, had taxed us severely. I now made the mistake of asking a further effort from the men, which they were rash enough not to refuse. For want of rope ladders – absolutely indispensable for such work – I had planned to be let down on the rope. As we were about to do this Cabalet objected that the rope was not strong enough. So we doubled it, and tied it under my arms. I was loaded with a bag containing the acetylene lamp and various impedimenta. I had on my old trench helmet in case of falling stones, an electric lamp in my hand and a whistle in my mouth. We arranged a system of whistle signals.

Then I slid over the brink of the abyss, as far as possible from the cataract, and my assistants let me down rapidly hand over hand. There was an overhang; I swung free in a void. The electric light showed me an ugly black wall, which I kicked at each swing of the rope, knocking off stones. Occasionally also I brushed the waterfall. I kept blowing the whistle to direct my descent.

At a depth of sixty feet I saw sticking out from the wall a little horizontal slab just big enough for my feet. I managed to get a foothold, whistled twice as a signal to stop, and perched on the terrifying balcony. Below me I could see nothing but the column of the waterfall, piercing the gloom to an unknown depth. I managed to kick down a big stone, which fell with the whistle of a cannon-ball to crash far below. Still I could not tell whether it had reached bottom or had merely struck an outcrop. In any case the rope would not reach that far; there was no use in descending further. For a long time I watched the plume of water roar from the top, where the men's lamps lit it up, to its disappearance in the depths.

I whistled three times, and then waited with muscles tensed for the hoist. The rope tautened and vibrated. I repeated the signal; the rope tautened still more, and I was raised a little. Now I could feel the trembling of the rope as it rubbed on the projection overhead. I began to revolve in space; then my upward movement stopped. I whistled; I felt a hesitation; I went up three feet. Then I went down six. I could see what was happening: the men above were exhausted, and my weight and the friction set their efforts at naught. I began to spin like a top. Now and then I dangled under the waterfall, which hammered me, and made me still heavier. I could have wished myself elsewhere!

I whistled frantically, but the rope must have been caught. Perhaps it was wearing through. I continued to dangle, as if hanged, in the abyss. By a desperate effort I managed to swing towards the wall. I tried to catch hold of it, but the wet, slippery rock offered no grip, and I dangled again at the end of my line.

I heard anguished voices; in every nerve I felt the frightful tension on the rope. Slowly, very slowly, I went up by short, feeble tugs. But I went up. There were long pauses, but gradually I neared the overhang, and at last my head rose over the edge. The overhang added to the friction, and there was another stop, during which I stared at the demon-faced figures struggling to wrench me from the abyss. Instinctively I looked at their shaking hands on the rope. There was a groan from Cabalet, one last yank, and I sprawled over the edge, landing on my knees at the feet of my exhausted saviours.

After resting from the worst of the shock and strain, we started for the surface. It took us three hours to cover that five hundred feet. The moonlight outside was magnificent. By the time we finished the endless descent to the works (bent double as we were under loads of stiff wet ropes) it was ten p.m., and there was considerable uneasiness over our absence.

The cavern was putting up a desperate resistance, but I would not own myself beaten. I returned to the assault with my wife and the two faithful porters. This time the generosity of the Academy of Sciences, the Touring Club de France, and the National Committee on Geodesy and Geophysics provided me with the equipment we had lacked. The tackle and ladders were made of rope and electrum, extremely light and thin. My friend, R. de Joly, president of the Spéléo-Club de France, and himself a great cavern-explorer, designed and built both this and a brilliant electric light worn on the forehead. Thus outfitted I was able to try again the terrifying descent of the last cascade.

I went down my rope ladder into the cold and brutal pounding of the cataract; the strong arms of the trio at the top kept me in leash on a 650-foot rope. I ducked my helmeted head between my shoulders, but the water blinded and choked me all the same. I touched an outcrop at 195 feet down, and then went on down a forty-five-degree shaft where the torrent foamed and leaped until I reached a new roaring, perpendicular drop. Here I found that my water-filled whistle had changed to a deeper note, and my assistants could not hear my signals. I had to climb up under great difficulties, braving the cold violence of the cataract, after reaching the respectable depth of 730 feet.

During all these explorations I had kept an eye out for geological and hydrological data; compass in hand, I had made a sketch-map, carefully recording depths and distances. I thus found that the cavern at 455 feet down was separated from the cliff outside by only 227 feet of rock. This was the answer to the problem of diverting the stream. But before the work began it was necessary to check up on my sketch, which, of course, was only an indication, though a careful one. It was decided to take very exact measurements, levels, and triangulations from inside and outside the cavern.

A young engineer, Monsieur C. Verchère, volunteered for the delicate and probably unprecedented task. We managed to carry it out successfully, always with the assistance of Cabalet and Lledo.

Five sessions of from eight to ten hours each were necessary, and one of them came close to catastrophe. The rock barrier which I had thought so dangerous on my first descent, and which we had eventually got used to, went down with a terrific uproar as we climbed it. Blocks of four or five cubic yards tumbled from all directions, and shattered in the bed of the stream. By a miracle nobody was injured, and we lost nothing but a little equipment, which was snatched from our fingers.

Our work confirmed my preliminary sketches as exactly as we could have wished. A horizontal tunnel 227 feet long, sunk from outside to the cavern, would divert the torrent to human use.

My task was finished. But during all my explorations I had never ceased to wonder whether the Cigalère cavern and the upper abyss were continuous. Exact altitude figures left no doubt of the cavern's importance. It was hopeless to try going deeper than 650 feet for the present; the waterfalls were too dangerous. I decided to wait until the proposed diversion tunnel was dug, and then to make another assault.

Meanwhile, it had been found that the tunnel could be sunk higher up, only 130 feet from the mouth of the natural shaft; the tunnel then had to be but 162 feet long.

On 20 November 1935 I learned that the tunnel was finished. I immediately organized a last expedition to profit by the stopping of the cascades. It was late in the season anyway; the Pyrenees were under heavy snow. But on the night of 20-21 November a raging tempest brought another snowfall. Luckily the miners had time to divert the stream into the tunnel before hastily abandoning the spot.

At daybreak of 22 November we set out for the upper shaft with my complete outfit, consisting, among other things, of 650 feet of rope ladder, 1,200 feet of rope, a collapsible air-filled canoe, and a telephone. The party consisted of my wife and me, Cabalet (to whom the chasm was an old friend), and four Basques, including Pierre Halcaren, a wonderful athlete and an absolutely devoted assistant. All five had volunteered, fully realizing the danger of our attempt, and they all shared our determination to start at the top and go all the way through to the bottom of the Cigalère.

We struggled up the steep mountain through three feet of snow. At eight a.m. we started down the cavern. A temporary bulwark of sandbags diverted the stream from the cavern to the outside. Unfortunately the bulwark leaked a good deal, and the cascades were not dry. They were much diminished, and we escaped the complete immersions of other years, but we were showered with water at thirty-five degrees Fahrenheit. When we went down the falls, the water would run down the sides of the rope ladders, into our sleeves, and come out in our boots. We were soon soaked through.

At noon we reached the point where I had gone down alone the year before. This time we had left two porters, Chouhourt and Phordoy, at a level spot 440 feet down; we stopped to rest on the black, shiny rocks at 500 feet. Here I fastened the end of a 260-foot rope to my belt. Then Cabalet, Halçaren, and Larraus let me down an interminable cascade, a sort of sixty-degree pitch interrupted by perpendicular drops. The water fell deeper and ever deeper ahead of me. On my way down I congratulated myself on having stopped when I did the year before; I should undoubtedly have been knocked out and drowned by the roaring cataract. To-day the trickle of the stream was but a petty annoyance, and I went down briskly.

Long whistles and a yank on the rope informed me that the latter was all paid out. There was nothing for it but to ascend, report my observations, and organize the descent to the new level. Before I started I was glad to notice that the cavern still yawned below me. The exploration looked most promising; but we had always to get down our spare equipment in its four enormous bags, made heavier by water.

My wife in turn went down to the length of the rope, and when she whistled to signal her safe arrival we prepared to join her with the bags. If we were to descend all the way to the Cigalère (which we began to think possible) we must not be stopped for want of tackle. We even let down the pneumatic canoe, in case of deep pools. As the stream had been diverted but twenty-four hours before, such basins might still stop us.

Our hand-to-hand struggles with the waterlogged bags were the greatest strain of this trip. Among other things we had to shore up a balanced boulder which rocked and threatened to crush us. Finally, we managed to join my wife, who had been waiting at the end of the rope for an hour.

Lower down, we had to wriggle through a section of upheavals; boulders were heaped and wedged in alarming positions along the tunnel. Below this plug in the passage, which we crawled through in fear and trembling, we were surprised to find that the cavern split. We followed one branch to a place where masses of still wet sand overlay a final crevice.

The second conduit was a low tunnel hollowed out of hard white limestone. We crawled down a sloping tube cluttered with round stones. At one point I had to remove a rock, and dig us a passage. We had temporarily abandoned the bags at the mouth of the tube. We crawled one after another, impatiently waiting for the ceiling to rise, and hoping to find a deep perpendicular shaft that would let us into the Cigalère cavern, which could not be far below.

Our wish was not fulfilled: Instead of the last precipice I encountered a low roof, where the water still hurried in. All I could do was to slide into the crack. To do this I had to undress completely, so as to make myself thin and keep from absolutely soaking my clothes. The party crawled backward to an opening where I could sit up to undress.

Even if I succeeded in forcing the passage there could be no question of getting my assistants or the equipment through. I sent them back with instructions to start up with the bags, while my wife and I crawled into the low tunnel again. I had the hardihood to struggle into the crack, lying flat in water at thirty-five degrees Fahrenheit; but my chest was ground into the brook-bed, the roof scraped my back, and my head got jammed. The fissure was impenetrable.

I backed up, shivering, and we sounded a retreat. The cavern had beaten us again. Among the tumbled boulders we caught up with the porters, whom we helped in their labour of Sisyphus with the bags. Climbing the rope ladders up the successive shafts, hauling the heavy sacks, grew more and more difficult; cold and hunger made the task worse. At the level spot at 440 feet, after a perpendicular climb of 200 feet, there was a general collapse. We soon spurred ourselves on by the sound of the *irrintzina*, the diabolical whinny of the Basques, and tremendous Ariège *anilhets*. In the echoing cavern these two undoubtedly prehistoric yells had a wild grandeur of their own.

It was eleven in the evening when we reached open air after fifteen hours' unbroken struggle with the cold black cavern. The night outside was black and bitter; a strong wind instantly blew out our lanterns. We stumbled along under our loads through the thick snow toward the works in the valley. Our bags and our clothes were solid ice. It was one a.m. before we could change, thaw out, and eat at the U.P.E. barracks.

Nineteen hours' hard work of seventeen people had gone to break the depth record among French caverns.

To give some idea of the scale of this cavern, I may say that the celebrated shaft of Padirac has a total depth of 325 feet. Several French caverns are deeper than this, and a few exceed 650 feet. These are the shaft of Hures and the Aven Armand, in Lozère, and the chasm of Rabanel in the Hérault, which vary from 650 to 680 feet; and the abyss of Heyle, in the Basque country. In July 1935 Max Cosyns, the stratosphere flier, and his friends Van der Elst and Pecher descended this abyss to a depth of 810 feet.

Our chasm in Ariège, with the communicating grotto of the Cigalère, totals 1,566 feet. We climbed 325 feet in the lower cavern, and our last descent into the upper one reached a depth of 979 feet. It thus stands comparison with the deepest chasms known, almost all of which are in Italy.

The king of them all is the della Preta chasm (Venezia). A group of Verona spelaeologists spent two years on it, and in 1927 reached bottom at 2,071 feet.

In 1934 other Italian explorers, after several years' work, descended to the bottom of the abyss of Corchia (Apuan Alps). It is 1,758 feet deep. In 1928 a group of Trieste alpinists ended three years' efforts by reaching the bottom of the abyss of Verco (Isonzo) at 1,683 feet. The same year another Trieste expedition went down 1,560 feet in the abyss of Montenero (Carniola).

These successive explorations have dethroned the terrible Bertarelli abyss (Istria), which reigned supreme until 1925 with 1,462 feet. The descents have been made by groups of Italian spelaeologists and alpinists elaborately organized and equipped; the work is dangerous and exhausting, and several bold pioneers have lost their lives in its course.

From the above list it is evident that the new chasm in the Pyrenees is among the world's deepest. But that fact means more than mere record figures or competition to get 'furthest down.'

The admirable explorations of the Italians have opened a new chapter in physical geography. Ten years ago no one suspected hydro-geological phenomena at such depths, and these phenomena have taken on an unquestionable general importance, raising puzzling but fascinating scientific questions.

All the great abysses have been found entirely choked. That which I had the luck to discover was the only one which still had two openings, and carried an active and permanent stream from top to bottom: it was the deepest negotiable hydro-geological penetration in the world. It illustrated perfectly, and on the largest scale known, the mechanism of underground water circulation; this, in turn, leads to other geological problems. Some phenomena of terrestrial morphology may be explained by the formation, age, and functioning of these caverns. At the bottom of the abysses, probably, is the answer to such questions as out-throws, movements of earth's crust, transgressions and regressions, the hollowing of valleys, glaciations, erosion cycles, and the drying up of streams. In the words of É.-A. Martel, they will explain 'an extent of denudation and surface changes which staggers the imagination and upsets many theories.' Between the Ariège chasm and the Cigalère cavern below, there was a distance of not more than twenty-six feet still to be explored. After the permanent masonry diversion of the stream was finished I renewed my efforts; I scaled another cascade in the Cigalère, and I did force the flat tunnel in the upper chasm, though I had to crawl by inches in the glacial water. The remaining distance is very short, but the cavern is not yet conquered.

I hope, before too long, to have a last, successful set-to with the great chasm, which I am happy to baptize the Gouffre Martel in honour of the great explorer and geologist who so often risked his life in forty-five years' explorations below ground.

PART FIVE

PUZZLES AND WONDERS BELOW GROUND

*

Felix qui potuit rerum cognoscere causas

VERGIL

I

THE STORY OF A RAINDROP

*

What can be harder than a rock? What softer than the drop
Which leaves its deep mark cut in stone?

OVID

*

IT rains. The water that falls will eventually reach one of
three destinations: it will trickle along the surface to join a
stream, and finally pour into the sea; about a third of all the
water that falls will evaporate, and form new clouds; and part
of the ground water will disappear underground. We have
seen how whole brooks and rivers are swallowed up by
cracks in their beds and by caverns and chasms.

Nearly always the water that disappears returns to daylight
sooner or later. In fact resurgences are more common than
disappearances, because the resurgences often collect the
seepage of a wide area.

The paths and functioning of subterranean watercourses
are now well understood. All abysses and caverns, even those
now dry, were hollowed out or at least shaped and enlarged by

water, and so the work of streams below ground is well worth study.

This is not the place to treat of the erosion, corrosion, and hydro-dynamic pressure which produce caverns; nor have I space to go into the fascinating but complicated subject of hot springs and vulcanology.

This chapter deals with a raindrop, so I shall consider not the noisy torrents rushing underground, but the water which seeps into the bosom of the earth. This water first soaks the soil, giving life to plants. Partly by capillary action it goes through cracks and chinks, pierces the soil layer, and reaches the underlying bedrock. Here begin the journey we shall follow and the transformations we shall watch.

In its journey from cloud to rock, through air and humus, the raindrop takes on a charge of carbon dioxide, forming a faintly acid solution. This acid dissolves an infinitesimal quantity of the limestone over which it passes. The drop seeps through the rock, and emerges after hours, days, or months to cling to a cavern ceiling. Here, exposed to air, it begins to evaporate, and thus to concentrate the calcium carbonate solution. Finally it falls, leaving a little of its carbonate on the ceiling. The carbonate crystallizes there in the form of calcite or calc-spar. Striking the floor, the drop spatters and leaves another trace of calcium carbonate where it hits.

The drops form not just anywhere, but at certain particular spots: cracks, fissures, and projections lead the water, like the drip from the edge of a roof. The drip of years, of centuries, of tens of centuries produces the curious crystalline formations called stalactites (hanging from the ceiling) and stalagmites (rising from the floor).

A stalactite in process of formation is much like an icicle, with the same pointed cylindrical shape. Stalagmites are usually squatter and less regular. When the drop falls from some height, two things may happen where it strikes. On a rock floor the drop spatters, producing a little mound, later to develop into a fat, irregular stalagmite. If the floor is earth, the drop bores a more or less cylindrical hole – one stage in the development of certain stalagmites. At a certain depth the drop loses its penetrative power, because the water collected in the miniature well breaks the force of the fall. Little by little the constant formation of calcite fills up the hole. Finally it is filled solid. Then the stalagmite begins to rise from the floor to meet the stalactite.

As stalactite and stalagmite grow, they come nearer and nearer, and finally join into a pillar between the cavern floor and ceiling. The drip is replaced by a trickle, covering the pillar with a film of water, and fattening it by continual deposit of calcium carbonate, which turns to calcite.

The varying sizes of stalactites and pillars are not, as was long believed, a sure clue to their age. Their growth is most irregular, subject to variable factors which defy all attempts at chronology based on size. Comparison between the rate of stalactite formation in caverns and on the roofs of artificial tunnels, viaducts, and the like makes the possible error obvious. The stalactites on man-made structures grow much faster because of quick evaporation in open air, and because cement charges the water with concentrated calcium carbonate. There are great variations, furthermore, between one cavern and another, sometimes between two chambers in one grotto. Varying rainfall is one cause; rainy countries produce more stalactites than do dry regions. The thickness of rock penetrated by the water is important: thin ceilings do not give the water enough precipitate for large stalactites. The calcium carbonate content of limestone varies greatly from one place to another. Changes in rainfall in the course of ages also have their effect. There are other causes more or less accidental: the drip may move, interrupting the formation of a stalactite; surface changes, such as a forest replacing a bare area, may affect the seepage.

Despite these obvious causes of error, the fact remains that a stalactite or stalagmitic deposit of any consequence is a matter of centuries. And though it is rash to say how many centuries, we can often tell that the deposit has been very slow. In the cavern of Montespan, for instance, it was the stalagmite which definitely proved the antiquity of the remains. Calcite deposits have filled the caverns with picturesque and truly magical formations, some of which are not yet understood. Besides stalactites, stalagmites, and their variants (pillars, curtains, petrified cascades, stalagmite floors and corridors, collectively called *dripstone*), there are yet more curious formations.

One of the most unexpected is floating calcite, which dulls the smooth surface of underground pools. At first glance it looks like dust; a second look shows it to be a thin film. It is calcium carbonate, which saturates the water of basins lacking an outlet. If water evaporates and the saturation increases, the film thickens and grows heavier, finally sinking in fragments to the bottom of the basin. Here the bits crystallize in the shape of enchanting little bouquets, white or lovely yellow, reminiscent of coral reefs. Capillary action tends to pile the floating calcite on the edges of the pool, producing ridges like those along the sea-shore. Variations in the water-level build the ridges into a sort of coping, and then into winding barriers. These irregular barriers are usually connected or tangent; they form a lovely pattern of compartments and hollows, each containing crystal-clear water, a miniature submarine landscape.

Mondmilch, or moon-milk, is a special state of calcite: stalagmite with too much water to solidify and crystalize. It thus remains in an amorphous, colloid state. It is a pure white paste, resembling white lead, and is found only in caverns whose air is saturated with moisture, allowing almost no evaporation. The paste smears the rugged stone, and fills up crevices.

Another formation due to underground water is the oolite, or cave pearl; it was once thought fabulously rare, but now is a well-understood natural curiosity, though an uncommon one. The first oolites I ever saw were in the Grotte de Cagire, whose exploration is described on an earlier page. In a basin of moderate depth, fed by a cascading thread of water, the agitation of the water keeps grains of sand in suspension. If the water has enough calcium content, and the stream is not too violent, these little fragments roll perpetually in the whirlpool, and gradually take on a limestone deposit. The hard deposit armours the kernel, and grows constantly thicker. The pearl, continually rolled about, becomes almost perfectly spherical and extremely hard. Starting with a grain of sand, an oolite may grow to the size of a pigeon's egg. Beyond this size the lump is too heavy to move in the water, and soon grows to the rock. A more violent whirlpool will not produce larger pearls, because if the water is too much disturbed the calcite cannot deposit itself.

If we saw an oolite through the centre, we find the kernel around which the pearl was formed, just as oysters form pearls around foreign bodies. Sometimes we find concentric coatings like tree rings. In oolites these coatings are due to interruptions in the deposit of calcite, or in other words to temporary stoppages of the cascade. Many cave pearls are dull and yellowish, but some are as white and shiny as porcelain.

In a few rare caverns there are extraordinary irregular stalactites, apparently defying the laws of gravity, and entirely apart from the usual blade shape; they are called helictites. The handsomest in France are in the grotto of the Grand Roc, near Les Eyzies (Dordogne), and the grotto of Courniou (Hérault).

Their chemical composition is that of ordinary stalactites, but the laws governing their formation and structure are almost a complete mystery. There are several theories, all quite possibly wrong. These stalactites are a flamboyance of nature; they are disconcerting and fairy-like, daring and fantastic. They are usually thin, almost thread-like, hanging vertically from the ceiling; suddenly, for no reason, they bend sharply, rise at an acute angle or in a spiral, fling out tentacles in all directions; they cling to neighbouring stalactites, only to free themselves again, and sometimes touch the ceiling from which they hang. Helictites, of course, are the work of calcium carbonate dissolved in water, but no one knows how the work is done. There has been talk of air-currents, of capillary or crystallization phenomena, of a colloid state. The most likely hypothesis seems to be that of some yet unexplained kind of osmosis. Osmosis in plants and colloid solutions is a displacement of molecules despite gravity and inertia.

But osmosis has been observed in only the animal and vegetable kingdoms; must we carry it over to the mineral kingdom, breaking down an otherwise inviolable barrier, and likening inorganic to organic cells?

The ancients imagined this possibility, and boldly took the step which gives us pause: they believed in a sort of mineral life. It may have been dream, ignorance, or prescience; but already we have had to return to such ancient concepts as transmutation and catalysis (from alchemy), and opotherapy (treatment with gland extract) in medicine. Must we explain helictites by the ancient and no doubt empirical concept of 'vegetation of minerals'?

Abbé A. Glory, a distinguished spelaeologist, has proposed an ingenious theory, too technical to explain here, based on laws of equilibrium, capillarity, and convection, and on evaporation, crystallization, and gravity.

Sometimes the water below ground is too swift to leave its calcite in the caverns, and so it drops the deposit outside, where evaporation is quicker. This produces *tufa*, or surface stalagmite, of which some vast accumulations exist. All springs with heavy calcium-carbonate content produce this porous stone.

The Fountain of Saint-Alyre at Clermont-Ferrand is famous; objects immersed in it soon become covered with calcite. 'Hard water' is merely water which has taken on calcium carbonate underground. Hard water eventually fills up watermains and plumbing. (The Roman aqueduct of Pont du Gard, for instance, has an enormously thick calcite deposit.) Kettles and double boilers filled with hard water become covered with a calcium-carbonate shell. Hard water prevents soap from lathering, hardens vegetables, and slows up their cooking.

Water dissolves, transports, and deposits in the caverns other substances besides calcite. Saltpetre, for instance, is a crystallized deposit of soil nitrates, produced by the decomposition of vegetable matter. Another such deposit is aragonite – magnificent crystals, flowers, needles, and flexible threads such as I found in the Grotte de la Cigalère. These offer a puzzle as complete as the helictites. The shrubs, crystal bushes, flowers, and cords, coloured by metallic sulphurs, must have complex and perhaps unknown chemical compositions. The cavern of the Cigalère is about 975 feet below a mine of blende and galena, and was undoubtedly hollowed out of the fault in the rock through which the vein of ore rose. The crystals may possibly be pseudomorphs (crystals consisting of one mineral, but having the form of another).

The power of water underground becomes even more impressive when we remember that the thousands of known caverns and chasms are but an infinitesimal fraction of those which exist, but which man will never find because they have no outlet to the upper air. Who can tell what physical and chemical laws may rule the fantastic concretions of the subterranean world, whose mere ante-rooms alone we can explore?

2

SUBTERRANEAN PHENOMENA

*

That man is wise who has learned the lessons
of nature
PINDAR, *Olympics*

*

BELOW ground everything seems to have come from another world, and surprises and hallucinations are constant. Some of these peculiar phenomena have been explained; others remain mysterious and confusing. This chapter tries to help straighten out the confusion of fact and theory.

Two acquaintances of mine, having gone a few yards into a cave, were dumbfounded to hear someone talking at the far end of the vestibule. They rushed out in fright. One of them told me about it, and insisted, despite my explanations, that he had heard a conversation. I visited the cave myself one day; stopping suddenly in the first chamber, I heard a voice – not a human voice, but the voice of a brook chattering and splashing along its rugged bed. 'Talking grottoes' are legion. They are due sometimes to streams, sometimes to air-currents, and occasionally have had unexpected historical importance.

In antiquity oracles were consulted on all occasions. The most famous and most revered were conducted by sibyls. The Cumaean sibyl was the most celebrated of all; in her trance she interpreted the noises of some underground stream or wind from the bottom of the cave where she lived. Oracular grottoes and springs existed everywhere, and in some countries they still do. Especially in Morocco there are caverns where people sleep in order to hear the noises, which are interpreted as oracles. One common belief there deals with a marriage procession which took refuge in a cave during a storm, and was turned to stone. From the mouth of the cavern one sometimes hears the songs and music of the procession.

These rumblings probably come from an underground stream which flows only after violent storms.

When we were exploring the Grotte de la Cigalère, my brother and I were stopped by a passage too small to crawl through. Beyond we heard the roar of a cascade which we had been trying to reach for some time. I came back later with two engineers and two miners, who were interested in putting the waterfall to work. It took about an hour to open up the descending hole, through which we heard the roar of the cataract. We were disturbed by a violent cold blast from the hole, and we heard the cascade so close to us that we tied a rope to whichever man was swinging the pick head down in the rat-hole. We were taking no chances of any one's falling into the water. We all guessed at the probable height and force of the waterfall. All five of us were specialists in hydraulic work; imagine our stupefaction then, on forcing the passage, to find no water at all! The characteristic roar of the cataract was an illusion, or rather we had confounded it for an hour with the roar of the air through the bottle-neck.

This is one sort of acoustical illusion. Mistakes of hearing are frequent and most disconcerting, since we rely on hearing more than on any other sense underground.

One day my brother and I were looking over the great lower hall of the Cigalère. We were rooted to the spot by a series of crashes which sounded as if the cavern roof was caving in. The menacing uproar was three times repeated; we crouched fearfully against a pillar, watching the ceiling, and waiting for it to open and crush us. When the noise stopped, we regained a little confidence, and decided to go on. An hour later we were having difficulties in the freezing torrent when the terrible crashes came again, with such violence that an earthquake seemed the only explanation. That evening we told our experience to the engineers of the Union Pyrénéenne Électrique, and learned that the noise had come from mines set off in a tunnel of the power project; the time of the explosion agreed with the moment when we heard it. When we compared a map of the region with a plan of the cavern, we found that the detonations had carried through 1,950 feet of solid rock.

Though sound is carried thus remarkably through the ground, it is quickly lost in a cavern. Talking from one end of a chamber to the other is often most annoying, for the syllables interfere, and multiple echoes overlap. The voice is quickly lost in vertical abysses; signals, whistles, or a portable telephone are necessary.

The drip from the ceiling often disturbs the crushing silence of caverns with strange music. I may mention one phenomenon, which I call the 'magic flute'. I have several times heard melodious tones underground – a well-modulated flute note, repeated at regular intervals. The sound is produced by drops of water falling from a height to a clay floor; they hollow out a deep, narrow tube, like a flute. Each time that a drop falls into the tube it compresses the air, which escapes with a whistle.

Again, large hollow stalactites in the shape of a curtain or a bell give a deep, sonorous note when struck. In the cavern of Gargas (Hautes-Pyrénées) there is a collection of such stalactites on which the old guide, Rème, used to play a beautiful carillon by striking them with a wooden bar. The waves of sound lasted long in the vaulted cavern. Many American caverns have such chimes.

I must also mention certain rumbling sounds which have often terrified the uninitiated, and which, I confess, routed me when first I heard them. The noises are deep and powerful, making the air tremble; and they are produced by nothing more than the flight of bats! Not even a colony of the creatures is necessary to unloose the roar. One lone bat beating its wings in a narrow tunnel or cul-de-sac will produce thunder.

At the risk of being disbelieved I will record a still more astonishing phenomenon. A friend and I were crawling flat on our stomachs in a tight tube. Crawling flat is the most wearisome of all exercises; prolonged, it becomes agonizing and exhausting, and frequent rests are necessary. During one of these rests we were both squeezed tight between floor and ceiling of a flat tunnel. Suddenly I noticed a very quick, staccato sound pounding my ears, and even making air and floor tremble. I called my companion's attention to it, telling him to lie still and listen. He was only fifteen feet behind, but heard nothing. Then I detected a sort of resonance from quick blows whose exact nature escaped me. Finally the mystery was explained: incredible as it seems, what I heard were the heart-beats of my exhausted companion. They were heavy blows, which I felt throughout my body by way of the hollow stalagmite floor. This acted as an amplifier, for my companion's chest was pressed to the ground. There was no possible doubt; we went so far as to count his pulse. If I had been a doctor, I could have given my friend a going-over with this natural stethoscope.

Hearing is not the only sense deceived underground; optical illusions are frequent. The slightest natural feature of a cave takes on measureless proportions: a shaft a few yards deep becomes a chasm, a modest chamber seems an enormous hall, a small pool looks like a lake. Apparently the surrounding blackness, scarcely dissipated by a lantern, makes us lose all sense of judgement and proportion, hiding everything we habitually use for comparison. The eye instinctively prolongs anything that disappears into the darkness, and the prolongation leads to exaggeration. People honestly trying to judge distances and dimensions underground always exaggerate enormously. Inexperienced visitors to caves often multiply the actual distance by ten. The optical illusion above-mentioned, the difficulties of progress over broken terrain, the bad light, the instinctive fear of getting lost, and the uneasy feeling of being in a new world all multiply time and distance; when one comes to measure, he finds he has taken a couple of feet for five yards. Even specialists are deceived, and have to take measurements.

Another common occurrence, not due to inexperience, is that of getting into water unexpectedly. Luckily this disagreeable surprise happens only in shallow water, which is perfectly clear and free of reflections, and so gives no sign of its presence. I remember one day jumping into a rock hollow, and landing in water up to my waist. In another grotto I had the habit of kneeling to drink from a shallow basin. One day I was accompanied by a friend, who tried to imitate me. I saw him bend over, and then start back, puffing noisily. Thinking to moisten his lips, he had submerged his whole face.

Deep water can be seen underground from some distance away; it looks black. In flashlight photographs the water of subterranean streams is dull and sombre, quite without beauty. Of course certain sea grottoes are exceptions, like the famous Blue Grotto of the Isle of Capri. There a peculiar play of light stains the water a fairy azure, and turns a submerged oar to living silver.

Beyond the realm of acoustics and optics there are many strange things below ground.

In the Ouled Ayach chasm in the Moroccan Atlas, 326 feet straight down, I crawled down a sloping tunnel, and found myself standing in an underground meadow of thick, luxuriant grass, every blade of it white or translucent. The albino vegetation rippled in the breeze, and its shoots turned towards a sun they would never reach.

The disposition of the chasm explained this natural monstrosity. The outer chamber, right at the bottom of the chasm, had received a stupendous cataract, and was bare and eroded. The second chamber, on the other hand, received the water only after the impetus was spent. Here were deposited all sorts of vegetable matter; chunks of turf, roots, driftwood, torn from the slopes above, formed a humus where countless seeds germinated and grew in perpetual dampness.

As I crawled onward, sinking into a spongy mess of vegetation which gave off stale, disgusting odours, I barely dodged an enormous warty toad (fit inhabitant of this nightmare meadow), which must have hatched from an egg washed down in some grass-tuft.

Unlike mine shafts and borings, natural caverns seem to be colder as they get deeper. In fact, the deepest natural cavities are among the coldest. This phenomenon may seem to upset the theory of radiation from the fiery centre of our globe, but

in reality it is due to free air-circulation in caverns. The circulation takes place not only through the orifices of the cavern, but
through fissures and faults in the limestone. Furthermore, the
streams that traverse the caves chill stone and air. The deepest
chasms known are in the mountains, where the water is cold,
and consequently the temperature at the bottom of these
chasms is from thirty-three to forty-three degrees Fahrenheit.

Such observations have disposed of the theory that the air
of caverns remains at a constant temperature of fifty-two
degrees. As a matter of fact there is not even a uniform temperature for any one cavern, let alone for caverns in general.
The thermometer underground varies according to season,
day and night, even time of day. These variations cause considerable air movements; the blowing tunnel in the Gouffre
Martel, for instance, took off our hats.

In natural vertical shafts, different temperatures inside and
outside make the air currents reverse their direction. In the
summer the currents usually go down, while in winter the
warmer air of the cavern rises out of the ground. If there is a
great difference of temperature (if it is freezing outside, for
instance), the air current steams.

These 'smoking holes' are often responsible for popular
fears of volcanoes. The same simple phenomenon occurs
with springs which are supposed to run hot in winter (because
they steam) and cold in summer. In reality they vary by only a
few degrees between the seasons. But obviously if the air is at
thirty-two degrees, and you dip your hand in a spring at
fifty degrees, you have a sensation of warmth; and if it is
120 degrees in the summer sun, water drunk at fifty or fifty-
four degrees will seem icy.

The warm air usually steams only at the mouths of shafts
and caverns, but sometimes this happens underground where
two air currents of different temperatures meet. The steam
was a great nuisance at one place in the grotto of Labastide.
When the blackness of a cavern is reinforced by thick mist,
one is lost in a moment.

The masses of ice sometimes found in chasms and caverns
were long a puzzle, but I think the puzzle is answered in my

earlier chapter on the Grotte Casteret. At the height of summer the air temperature there is below thirty-two degrees Fahrenheit, and wet boots freeze hard as one walks.

All this proves the free air-circulation in caverns. It is a mistake to think that air is vitiated and unbreathable the moment one gets below ground. Of course there are exceptions, just as there are on the surface. Certain gorges, caverns, and chasms are filled with dangerous gas, usually carbon dioxide. At the famous Death Valley in the Yellowstone, carbon dioxide and hydrogen sulphide issue from cracks in the rock, killing animals that venture near. One of the oldest known grottoes having this peculiarity is the Solfatara of Puzzola, near Naples. (The dictionary defines a solfatara as 'a volcanic vent, from which only sulphurous exhalations and aqueous vapours are emitted, encrusting the edge with sulphur and other minerals.') This is a very small cavern hollowed in the lava of Vesuvius. It was used in antiquity as a Turkish and hot bath, as certain arrangements show. The high temperature and sulphurous vapours prevent complete exploration, which would probably reveal a vertical chimney.

The Grotte de Saint-Mart at Royat, a bigger one, has been known since 1786, and exploited as a curiosity since 1875. It is famous for producing carbon dioxide, whose level varies with the barometric pressure. In winter, when the temperature reaches twenty-three degrees Fahrenheit, the production of gas stops. The cavern of the Creux du Souci is a chasm sixty-five feet deep in the lava of the Puy de Montchal, in Auvergne; barometric pressure here makes the depth of carbon dioxide vary from a foot or so to sixty-five feet. Of course the layer of gas grows thicker as the pressure decreases. Similar caverns whose emanations are volcanic in origin are very plentiful.

Far more puzzling and dangerous are the carbon-dioxide pockets which one finds in certain limestone caverns, far from any volcanic centre; they are quite impossible to foresee. Unexpected carbon dioxide is a formidable danger in underground exploration, for one may be suddenly overcome, and quickly asphyxiated. Noxious gases are quite rare, but all the more dangerous for that reason. I myself have had the agonizing feeling of suffocation but twice. In the cavern of Arbon (Haute-Garonne) I pushed forward despite the guttering of my acetylene lamp and a perceptible difficulty in breathing. I was inexperienced at the time, and the result was an attack of fever with violent headache and nausea. I was in bad shape and much weakened by the time I got out of the cavern. My other encounter with gas, in the grotto of Labastide, I have described on an earlier page. I may remark in passing that the use of electric light below ground combines with other inconveniences the serious defect of not revealing carbon dioxide when present.

The formation of carbon dioxide in caverns far from any volcanic or thermal region still puzzles us. In many cases, of course, the gas is not carbon dioxide, but some other noxious vapour produced by decomposition, as at Labastide. The Grotto of the Fairies at St Moritz (Switzerland) contains a gas which puts out flames, but does not asphyxiate. In the main corridor, 1,950 feet from the entrance, the lights suddenly go out, but one still breathes, though with difficulty. The difficulty produces fever and sweating. Analysis of the air from the cavern shows 1.99 per cent of carbon dioxide. The grotto of Büdösbarland, in Transylvania, on the other hand, has an atmosphere consisting of 95.49 per cent carbon dioxide, and, needless to say, has never been explored. All these gases are doubly dangerous because vagrant; they move about from year to year, and turn up where they have never been noticed before.

There are interesting barometric variations underground. In 1904 E. Rahir noticed strange disturbances of his barometer in a huge Swiss cavern, the Höll-Loch. Near a 130-foot cascade the needle of the instrument jumped violently. In 1908 É.-A. Martel noticed similar variations close to the waterfalls in the Basque gorges of Holçarte and Cacouette. I myself noticed beside the falls in the Gouffre Martel that my altimeter went wild, as it did in the wind-hole of the Cigalère.

Evidently subterranean cascades and air-currents compress or rarefy the air, falsifying barometric data.

Prolonged simultaneous recordings in open air and at the

bottom of deep caverns have also shown that variations of atmospheric pressure are slightly accentuated underground. The cause of the difference is unknown. The curious experiments of Messrs Idrac and de Pontbriand in the blowing wells of the Caux country showed that barometers installed in the opening of the wells indicated changes several hours before the recording barometers placed beyond the shafts' influence. The peasants would study the strength and direction of the wind coming from these artificial cavities in order to judge weather probabilities.

When sketching the Grotte de la Cigalère by compass we were surprised to find our plan assuming a shape entirely improbable and contrary to our sense of direction. Even though my sense of direction might be weakened by several hours' turning about below ground, I could believe in no such complete contradiction between compass and instinct. I suspected the instrument, and, in fact, soon discovered that the compass had gone crazy. I discovered later that I had been sketching 975 feet below the Sentein mines, probably right in the vein which fed them.

It will surprise no one that metal-bearing rock should deflect the compass. But some of the magnetic phenomena which have been observed are really astonishing.

Dr E. Mathias, a physician of Toulouse, has plotted the magnetic map of various parts of France, and has shown that the terrestrial magnetic field on the earth's surface is streaked with telluric currents passing from west to east. Sudden irregularities in the surface, such as deep gorges, and even caverns and underground rivers, disturb and deflect these currents.

There are also magnetic springs – waters containing a high proportion of carbonic acid and a heavy deposit of magnetic iron. A steel blade can be magnetized simply by dipping it in the water; a compass held over the water is immediately deflected. When the production of carbonic acid ceases, the water loses its magnetism. Such springs exist at Catersburg Springs, Lebanon, and Fort Wayne, Indiana.

Magnetic springs bring us to radioactivity. Experiments by Elster and Geitel show that air from the earth and inside caverns is radioactive. Brunhes and David have explained the enormous ionization of the air in caverns. Recently the distinguished naturalist Bouget, with Director C. Dauzère of the Pic du Midi Observatory, showed that because of ionization cavern and chasm openings attract lightning. Having assisted in the work of Messrs Bouget and Dauzère, I can testify that trees and boulders on the edges of chasms are blasted with astonishing frequency.

Water coming from the depths of the earth, especially thermal and mineral water, has radioactive properties; underground streams also are radioactive, and there is strong ionization at their resurgences.

These observations show that radium or some other analogous substance still unknown exists almost everywhere underground, impregnating air and water. In support of this theory I may mention the spring of Clitunno, near Spoleto (Umbria). It is magnificently rainbow-tinted, and its water has radium's property of slowly staining glass violet. It is probable that the water contains infinitesimal radium particles.

Now we come to some hydraulic phenomena. Everyone knows of intermittent springs, the mechanism of whose periodic flow is an old and interesting puzzle. One of the most famous in France is that called the Fountain of Fontestorbe, in Ariège. It is the resurgence of a considerable stream, which functions for several months of the year in very curious fashion. It comes out of a small cave, which one can enter dryshod during the interval. The intermission lasts exactly thirty-two minutes and thirty seconds; then the water comes noisily out through a fissure to fill the cave for thirty-six minutes and thirty-six seconds. The flood takes fifteen minutes to reach its highest level; for four minutes it pours over a natural barrier; then the level sinks until the stream stops, and the grotto is dry. The resurgence pours out an average of 396 gallons per second. Many intermittent springs have monthly, daily, or hourly intervals (geysers, of course, are familiar), but few are so regular and rhythmical as the Fountain of Fontestorbe, which documents show has not varied in more than two centuries.

The chasm of Génerest (Hautes-Pyrénées) is an oval hole

100 by 35 feet, and 109 feet deep. É.-A. Martel discovered a strange pulsation in the water which fills the lower fifty feet of the chasm. The water rises thirteen feet in fifteen minutes, stands still three minutes, and takes forty minutes to go down to its original level. It rises again without a pause.

A theoretically possible explanation, and probably the correct one, is that a series of reservoirs fed by siphons of varying diameter causes the various intermittences. We shall have to be satisfied with this theory for the present, since no one has yet succeeded in penetrating an intermittent system.

I have been intimately concerned with another kind of daily variation in flow. At ten o'clock one morning in the underground torrent of the Grotte du Toro (Maladetta massif) I was surprised by swiftly rising water. I had to beat a hasty retreat to avoid drowning in the low tunnels of the cavern. The flood was due to the melting of the nearby glaciers which feed the stream. Every day at the same hour the sun starts the thaw, which produces variations of twenty-six to thirty-two feet between morning and evening levels at the Trou du Toro downstream. I managed to escape the daily floods by exploring at night, when the chill largely stopped the melting of the glaciers. Even so, it was more than exciting to crawl up rat-holes still dripping from the torrents of the day.

The menace of these sudden inundations to men who go far up underground streams can be imagined. Far from the outside world, absolutely ignorant of possible rains and storms, one risks being swept away by the torrent, drowned in low tunnels, or obliged to scramble up the walls out of reach of the flood. Some explorers have been thus surprised in uncomfortable and alarming positions, and imprisoned from a few hours to several days. Count Begouen and his sons were prisoners for a whole night in the Tuc d'Audoubert, waiting for the flood to subside. R. de Joly and several of his colleagues had some terrifying hours 325 feet below ground in the chasm of Paradis (Jura), at the foot of a waterfall suddenly swelled by a violent storm. In the Lürloch (Styria) seven persons, surprised by a sudden inundation which blocked a siphon, remained prisoners for a week. They were finally freed by a party under the spelaeologist Putick, who succeeded in opening up the siphon.

On another occasion some Italian explorers, 1,300 feet down in the Bertarelli abyss, were told by portable telephone that a violent storm was lashing the neighbourhood. Despite the warning a waterspout from the huge outer funnel of the chasm caught two of the explorers hastening up the rope ladders. They were hurled into the abyss, and killed. Several others took refuge on ledges, where they spent agonized hours waiting for rescue.

The suddenness of these subterranean freshets is equalled only by their violence and undreamed-of proportions. In certain chasms serving as man-holes along an underground stream the high water is tremendous. The river has been known to rise 115 feet above low water in the Padirac shaft. At the Ragas de Dardenne, near Toulon, a rise of 195 feet has been observed. It was the blast of rising air from such a freshet that caused the discovery of the chasm of Trebiciano (Istria). The chasm is 1,140 feet deep, and water-marks have been found from a 520-feet freshet. The bottom of this abyss is a large cavern which fills entirely at each flood of the Recca; its capacity is estimated at 55,000,000 gallons.

Following violent storms or long rainy spells underground freshets sometimes break into systems of tunnels rarely invaded by water. This produces temporary resurgences, which function but two or three times a year, sometimes less often. There are even caverns which have never spouted but once in the memory of man.

In the Grotto of the Goueil de Her (Haute-Garonne) one can usually walk dry-shod, but sometimes it vomits a jet of water with a dull roar and a loud detonation. This 'cannon-shot' phenomenon is rare, but well enough understood: it is caused by the sudden rise of the water, which compresses and expels the air.

Some natural wells, ordinarily dry, begin to give water in rainy weather. Some alternately emit and absorb water. Many lakes, and even the sea floor, have cracks, funnels, and conduits; they absorb the water, and dry up the lake, or feed it until it overflows. Lake Chad, which is subject to great variations of level, seems to be fed and emptied in this fashion.

The most extraordinary example known is Lake Alachua, near Gainesville, Florida. In 1823 the future lake was a meadow, bisected by a brook which went down a hole. In 1868, following heavy rains, the disappearance of the brook was blocked, and a sheet of water temporarily submerged the meadow. In 1873 there was a new obstruction; the water rose for several years, until the lake was twelve and one-third miles long. A steamboat line plied on it for fifteen years. In 1889 the water began to go down, and by 1891 the lake had entirely disappeared.

Among other extraordinary behaviour of water in caverns, alternations of the current remain unexplained. One case, that of the Inversac of Thau pond (*inversae aquae*, reversed waters), is a complete mystery: the pond alternately gives out fresh water and draws off brine.

Along with these phenomena I may mention the common one of submarine springs, particularly frequent in the Mediterranean. The island of Bahrein in the Persian Gulf has no fresh water, and swimmers take advantage of a spring in the sea floor by diving down the rising fresh-water current, which they capture in leather bottles.

Finally, to make an end of underground phenomena, there is a popular belief that certain springs weaken or dry up when it is about to rain. This seems like nonsense, but is proved by actual observation. Variations in atmospheric pressure do have an effect on the flow of springs. Even during droughts some springs run faster with a rising barometer. When the barometer falls, announcing rain or storm, they run more slowly, and may even stop altogether. The phenomenon has been noticed in the spring at the bottom of the Gouffre de Padirac, 325 feet below ground.

With all I have said in this chapter, I am far from having exhausted subterranean phenomena. I have not even finished with spelaeology – the study of natural cavities accessible to man – but other subjects demand our attention.

3

THE FAUNA OF CAVERNS

*

Natura maxime miranda in minimis

*

ONE question is often asked: 'What is there underground? Beasts, I suppose?' Apparently the idea of caves calls up all kinds of bizarre and repulsive animals. Reptiles, being supposed to inhabit dark, wet holes, play a large part in people's imagination, and no one likes the idea of meeting a snake in a cave. At the risk of shattering his illusions, let me assure the reader that the class of Reptilia has no underground representative.

Although I do not intend this chapter to be rigidly zoological, I must divide the inhabitants of caverns into two classes: *cavernicolous*, born, living, and dying underground, and *cavernophilous*, temporarily or accidentally living in caves.

Among the latter we have in France, in order of size, the bear, the badger, the fox, the marten, the cat, a few small carnivores, and the rabbit; among birds are the horned owl, the long-eared owl, and the screech-owl.

These creatures sometimes make their lairs in small tunnels not far from the mouths of caverns. In grottoes, not far in (but sometimes in deep galleries), one often finds tracks, beaten trails, claw-marks on the stone, and beds hollowed in the earth.

The bear is the largest cavernophilous animal in France. Although the brown bear no longer exists in the French Alps, some are killed every year in the Pyrenees; they hibernate in caverns at an altitude of 3,300 to 5,000 feet. The bear does not, as is sometimes said, go to sleep for a long period; it dozes and vegetates, living on the fat it has accumulated during the autumn. Its vital processes slow up, and it does not eat.

Hibernation apart, the bear frequents caverns, and often goes far below ground. In the Massif d'Arbas I once happened to see a bear-hunt in which a pack of dogs stopped at the mouth of a cave, yapping madly, but not daring to go in. As the hunters were no bolder than the dogs, the hunt ended there. Apparently this was not the first time that the wily bear had taken refuge in that cavern.

Although I have never had the misfortune to confront a live bear underground, I have often found skeletons, some evidently dead by mischance, others apparently animals which had retired to a cave to die.

Another frequenter of caverns is the badger, which digs deep burrows. It is fond of the narrow tubes and corridors of caves, where it finds an even temperature and the calm which seems to be the badger's chief interest. Tracks in damp earth have often told me of a badger in a cave, and one day as I wriggled painfully along a narrow tube I had the disagreeable surprise of coming nose to nose with a badger at bay in the cul-de-sac. He was as displeased as I, but determined to fight to the last. Having only a lamp to his strong jaws and sharp claws, I backed up as fast as I could go, leaving him to an uncomfortable retreat which was his by prior right anyway.

There is nothing worthy of special remark about the fox. In dry, earth-floored caves it digs a sort of nest lined with grass and leaves, where it deposits its litter of cubs. These nests harbour innumerable fleas, which, of course, begin to starve the moment the nest is abandoned. A man or animal crawling through the tunnel a few months later is instantly covered with famished parasites.

Several times I have had the disagreeable experience of saving flea colonies from starvation.

I have always been interested by the large number of cat skeletons in caves. Are they domestic or wild cats? I have found skeletons in caverns so far from human habitation that I do not think domestic cats would venture there; besides, why should they all die during one chance distant reconnoitre? Apparently wild cats are more numerous than is usually supposed. The skeletons, and particularly the skulls, bear no traces which would lend support to the theory that these were domestic cats dragged off and eaten by other animals.

Cavernophilous animals in other countries include the panther, the hyena, the jackal, and especially the porcupine, which lives underground all day, coming out only at night.

The jackdaw is particularly fond of mountain cavern-mouths. The mountaineers of the central Pyrenees, oddly enough, call the bird *cigale* (properly a cicada), and *cigalères* are rock cliffs frequented by jackdaws. It was thus that the Grotte de la Cigalère came by its name. The jackdaws nest in holes in the ceiling as far as 100 feet from the entrance.

To one who understands them, jackdaws are excellent indicators of caves and chasms. The ease and boldness of their flight is admirable; watching them carefully, one may see them circle some point, then fold their wings, and dive perpendicularly, to disappear in the ground. This is the proper moment to steer for the spot. Usually one finds a pit in the limestone. I have spent days watching the flight of jackdaws, and letting them discover chasms for me. On the steep slopes of the Mail de Bulard (Ariège) the jackdaws, watched through a glass, showed me several deep shafts with narrow mouths which otherwise I could never have spotted.

Jackdaws go down deep shafts so narrow that I have seen the birds unable to fly directly back from the bottom to the mouth. They climbed like autogyros, by short, steep flights, perching on every projection of the rock, rising little by little with loud noises of scraping wings. It is hard to say what attracts the birds to such inaccessible shafts; since jackdaws are not carnivorous, it cannot be the carcasses often found below.

Jackdaws even nest in chasms, and so have to feed their young much longer than if the eggs hatched above ground; the young birds are long unable to fly perpendicularly like their parents. At the bottom of narrow shafts I have found fully fledged young jackdaws, quite able to fly horizontally, still waiting for strength to make their first flight towards daylight. Occasionally I have taken little jackdaws to the surface, where they seemed much annoyed and dazzled by the unaccustomed sun. I once found a nest with eggs 200 feet straight down. In order to feed their young the birds descend and ascend at great inconvenience, sometimes twenty-five times an hour, as I noticed on one occasion. At each trip the bird can carry but one grasshopper, snail, or myrtle-berry to his hungry and well-grown brood.

All that I have said so far refers to cavernophilous fauna. One animal may serve to bridge the gap between cavernophilous and cavernicolous creatures – the bat, which lives in caves for months, but goes out during the pleasant season.

I shall take this opportunity to put in a good word for the bat. Bats are no longer so much persecuted as they once were, but many people feel for them an unreasoning physical repulsion, and consider the bat hideous, disgusting, and dangerous. This shows poor observation, or none at all. People never see bats close to, partly because the creatures are nocturnal, and thus some gross errors gain currency.

The bat is commonly thought of as a sort of naked, winged mouse, with claws by which it catches in people's hair. As a matter of fact, the bat has fine, soft fur, and its fragile little claws are used only to hang by on rock walls. The timid creatures do not dare come near man, let alone cling to his hair, and they fly so marvellously that there can be no question of accidental entanglement.

Visitors to bat caves sometimes notice a musky odour, and assume that bats have an unpleasant smell. But effect must not be taken for cause. Bat guano, enormous quantities of which exist in some caves, does have a disagreeable though by no means insupportable smell; but the bat itself is perfectly clean and odourless, as anybody can see by taking one in his hand.

But it may still be objected that the wings are naked and dreadful. Naked they are, true enough; but they are not dry, dead, or parchment-like. They are silky, translucent, filled with fine blood-vessels and nerves; the flexible bony structure is an absolute marvel.

Quite apart from any personal attractions the bat is very useful, and should be protected and cherished. All the twenty-five varieties living in France are exclusively insectivorous.

The execution which these active and voracious creatures do among insect pests can be imagined. But the bat does more than destroy myriads of insects; the waste from digesting them accumulates in caverns as guano. The guano deposits sometimes grow large enough to be exploited for agricultural purposes. Of all animal manures bat guano is the richest in fertilizing matter, especially in nitrogen and phosphoric acid.

Certain caverns are regular bat-guano mines. Cibolo Cave, a small cave in Texas, shelters a vast number of bats, and yields seventy tons of guano annually. The caverns of Carlsbad, New Mexico (probably America's most extensive caverns), have already yielded 100,000 tons. There are 260 varieties of bat in the United States, and in Texas regular bat 'farms' have been started. They are artificial shelters, a sort of high, wooden towers, where the bats have darkness, quiet, and suitable perches. The towers are inhabited by 6,000 to 10,000 bats at a time, yielding about two tons of guano annually. The guano sells at ten cents a pound in ten-pound bags.

As a matter of fact the bat shelters were not built for commercial purposes; Dr Charles A. R. Cambell, of San Antonio, hoped to combat the yellow-fever mosquito by attracting bats to the area ravaged by the disease. The bats do not yet seem to have exterminated the mosquito, but the guano has produced considerable revenue.

Although the bat in France is an unmixed blessing, I must admit it is not so everywhere. Certain tropical species eat more fruit than insects, and the large 'flying fox,' or fruit-bat, marauds orchards and banana plantations. There are also blood-drinking vampires, whose misdeeds have, however, been much exaggerated by travellers.

Having preached my fondness for the bat, I will try to show what the feeling is founded on, describing how bats act underground, and why they deserve so prominent a place in a chapter on cave fauna.

The bat is descended from strange animals that lived in the warm, uniform climate of earlier geologic ages; it has never been able to adapt itself to climatic changes, and, like many laggards in the animal kingdom, it has had to hibernate in caves. The caves have a fairly constant temperature, and the bats fall into prolonged lethargy.

Everything about bats is strange, even the way they perch and sleep. They hang by the feet, head down, bodies carefully enveloped in long, folded wings; they remain thus in the silence of the caverns from October to April. Their gregarious instinct leads them to pack into tight swarms for protection against chill and dampness, sometimes thousands of individuals together. But the protection is not enough; the bats' animation is suspended for months, and the creatures take on the temperature of the surrounding air. Of course, the bat is a warm-blooded animal, and in winter it is surprising to pick one up, hanging shrivelled like a dried fig, and feel how cold it is.

The bats sleep so soundly that one can detach and handle them without their showing any signs of life beyond shivering wings and a plaintive little cry. Water and even fire will not always rouse them. This lethargy does not last all winter, or at least is not continuous; bats are found flying around in caves even in mid-winter. Their mating is known to take place at that season, for the young are born in April, just when the creatures start hunting outside the cave at night again.

Considering their hard and complicated life, we should not expect bats to be prolific. Only one young one is the result of their nuptial flight in the gloom – a flight never yet surprised by man. The young one is naked and blind for several weeks, during which it clings with tiny claws to the mother; its mouth never releases her nipples, and she carries it everywhere, both flying and at rest.

We may well wonder how the bat can fly in the absolute darkness of caves, dodging obstacles and penetrating the uttermost depths. Its tiny eyes, lost in the fur, can hardly be very useful, yet on dark nights it catches infinitesimal insects in full flight. What sense takes the place of defective sight? Do bats perceive radiations unknown to us? As the fearful and wonderful convolutions of their noses show, bats have a keen sense of smell. Their ears are also very complicated; the outer ear consists of a double pinna, the smaller part of which serves by turns to close the ear and to amplify sound.

Bats no doubt perceive smells and sounds which we do not. As for touch, it seems to be their basic sense. The enormously long phalanges forming the wing-structure serve as tactile antennae. Probably by air disturbances felt through the wings the bat perceives and dodges such obstacles as stalactites.

Bat flight seems to us erratic and clumsy. I believe this is because bats move so swiftly that the eye does not follow every motion, and because we do not know why they dodge so. They flit about apparently at random in the moonlight to pursue insects, which they swallow in full flight; in fact bats fly with open mouths, like the swallow and the goatsucker, whose dizzying zigzags also are made in pursuit of insects.

Bats fly with a precision far beyond that of any bird. I am for ever astonished at the way they flit about in small caves without touching. I have disturbed them in tight corridors where I could barely wriggle through, yet despite their obvious fright they flew between my face and the wall, skimming but not touching me. My lamp did not blind them in the least. I have seen bats fly between ceiling and water of an underground stream where there was clearance of but a few fingers' breadth; they did not ripple the water or touch the rock. The only time when a bat is clumsy is when forcibly awakened from hibernation; then it flies little and badly, and soon falls. This must be the origin of our belief in bats' clumsiness.

I have occasionally tamed and raised bats – an easy matter. Their behaviour when released in a room is interesting to watch. Birds, not seeing the glass, would stupidly fly at the windows, and kill themselves. Not so the bats: they made a careful survey of the room, beginning close to the ceiling. They flew around and around, each time a little lower, until they skimmed the floor, flying between chair-legs and under sideboards without bumping. Not until they had finished their inspection would they stop to hang from a picture-frame or a cornice. No bird could have approached the performance. And the bat flies equally well by daylight, in darkness, or in the blinding glare of electric light.

The bat was long considered a sedentary creature, living in

one cave, and seldom emerging except for a little while at night. But these strange animals seem made to astonish naturalists to the last: a few species are sedentary, but, when winter comes on, others migrate tremendous distances. The experiment of banding bats' legs, as has been done with birds, has yielded astonishing facts. Certain vespertilionids, common in France during the summer, are not to be found in winter, even in caves. Where do they go in the cold season? They are found nowhere in Europe.

Banding gave the answer: to Japan!

I hope I have said enough to let the reader share my interest in bats; now we descend to the world of shades, there to see the pariahs of creation, the purely cavernicolous animals. Caverns and the lower depths of the ocean were both long thought bare of life; no living creature, it was supposed, could adapt itself to a habitat so completely different from our own. Students claimed that life could not exist without light, and specifically that there were no living organisms in the sea below 975 feet, the limit of solar penetration. But the first submarine explorations, from 1868 to 1870, disproved these theories, and opened the door to the fertile and fascinating science of oceanography. We now know that life abounds at every depth.

A hundred years earlier, in 1768, the first cavernicolous animals had been discovered by the scientist Laurenti. Oddly enough, he stumbled at once on the strangest of all, a *Proteus*. This is a sort of colourless salamander which lives in the underground waters of certain Austrian caverns; it may be as much as a foot long, with the body of an eel and four tiny legs. It is amphibious, having persistent gills for life under water and lungs to breathe air. Condemned to absolute darkness, it is not merely blind, but quite without eyes. Seven different species are known.

Later researches showed that the proteus was no unique monstrosity; the caves harboured an unsuspected abundance of life. There are protozoans, molluscs, crustaceans, insects, batrachians, twenty-three kinds of fish, and one mammal.

This is not the place for a systematic discussion of subterranean fauna, the less so because the biology of the underground realm is still very poorly understood; but some generalities do hold.

All these creatures have eyes wholly or partially atrophied; the organs of sight are useless in the dark, and so they disappear. The blindness is compensated for by extraordinary development of hearing, smell, and touch. Ordinary observation shows this to be true of hearing and smell, while the development of touch organs is characteristic. Cavernicolous animals have hypertrophied antennae, feelers, hair, or tentacles, all exquisitely sensitive.

Albinism, or lack of pigment, is another result of life in the dark. The fact itself is well known, and is evidently due to the fact that the animal absorbs no light; but no satisfactory explanation has yet been offered.

We might easily suppose that cave creatures would have phosphorescent organs like the luminous eyes of certain deep-sea animals. But with one exception underground zoology has shown nothing of the sort; apparently cavernicolous animals are sufficiently adapted to darkness for them to do without. There is also the question of possible radiations underground, imperceptible to human beings, but enabling other animals to get about in the dark. Recent infra-red-ray discoveries makes this plausible. It is known that ants, which live largely underground, can perceive ultra-violet rays.

Except for certain cave mosses which shine with a lovely emerald green, there is but one phosphorescent animal in caverns: a thread-shaped worm which lives in tightly-packed colonies of unnumbered individuals, hanging from the ceiling of the cavern of Waitomo, New Zealand. These glow-worms give enough light to read by, but at the slightest noise they pull in, and lose their luminosity. Apparently the phosphorescence is perfectly useless, for the worms are a low, eyeless form of life.

Cavernicolous fauna is more varied than we usually suppose; the Mammoth Cave in Kentucky alone has yielded more than a hundred species.

It is true that these are largely lower orders of life, but there are some vertebrates – blind fish, and one lonely mammal, a blind rat.

This rat, the *Neotoma*, lives in a few American caverns; it has highly developed whiskers. Despite its blindness it has eyes, which oddly enough are hypertrophied. This hypertrophy is not the only apparent contradiction to the common rule of blindness in cavernicolous species. The theory is that the *Neotoma* took to cave life at a period too recent to lose its eyes. The organs are still in the period of struggle and reaction against the dark.

One of the most embarrassing puzzles in subterranean zoology is the origin of cavernicolous fauna. This fauna was once supposed to have been specially created for life in the dark. Plain signs of evolution destroyed that theory, and now the question is how the animals became established below ground, and when.

Caves are undoubtedly populated in many ways: it is easy to imagine cases of animals or eggs carried below ground; running water has always been an important factor.

So far as the time is concerned, recent discoveries make it seem likely that we must go back to the tertiary era. Some cavernicolous species recall fossil animals which have been gone from the earth's surface for millions of years.

Who knows? Some day a biologist may yet penetrate the mystery of these pariahs of creation and their wonderful senses. Here may be methods of giving the deaf their hearing, of making the blind to see. Let us not forget the wings of the humble bat, which inspired the first attempts at flying-machines. Who knows what these underground studies may disclose?

PART SIX

DISCOVERY OF THE TRUE SOURCE OF THE GARONNE

*

Cascades that fall from the shifting snows,
Springs, torrents, brooks, and freshets of the Pyrenees . . .
DE VIGNY, *Le Cor*

I

BELOW GROUND IN THE ACCURSED MOUNTAINS

*

Thence issuing we again beheld the stars
DANTE, *Inferno*, Canto xxxiv

*

IN May 1928, my mother, my brother Martial, my wife, and I climbed Mont Néthou. It was our first reconnoitre in the Maladetta massif, where we planned more extensive work for a few months later.

Unexpected circumstances during the summer reduced our family troop to the limit; I began my annual campaign alone, with a subsidy from the Academy of Sciences 'to pursue my spelaeological work and investigations in the Pyrenees.' For days I made harassing marches in all directions, scanning rocks and cliffs, investigating fissures and chasms; night after night I slept under the open sky, sheltered by a boulder or a tree.

Finally I headed for a cavern which I found through the glass. This cavern penetrates the limestone slope of the Escaleta, the beginning of the Plan Ayguallud, at 6,890 feet. It was visited by Émile Belloc in 1897, though only in part, as I learned later. The mouth is some twenty feet above the bed of the Rio de la Valleta de Venasque, which joins the torrent of the Barrancos lower down to feed the Trou du Toro chasm.

Belloc recorded his visit to the cavern in a story in the French Alpine Club year-book for 1897. He estimated that he and two guides had covered 650 feet; yet his description shows that they stopped at a hole 'emitting an icy wind, and so small that a man could scarcely move in it', which is exactly 180 feet from the entrance. I mention this mistake of quadruplication only to show how, with the best will in the world, one is likely to exaggerate distances underground.

Soon reaching the 'narrow opening' where Belloc has turned back, I went to work to force the bottle-neck. I was sure that the violent blast coming out was a sign of great cavities beyond. I could not keep the candle lit in the wind, so I lay flat on my stomach in pitch darkness, and scooped up pebbles and wet gravel by the handful. After half-an-hour's frantic work clearing the wind-hole, crawling with care to avoid a cave-in, I reached the top of a cone of debris with a brook cascading down. Straightening up, I entered a magnificent new part of the cavern.

It was a huge, high-roofed rotunda. Here the continual murmur which I had heard while burrowing rose to a roar. I bent over the crack whence the noise came, and found there was a cascade thirty-five or fifty feet below.

I explored further corridors and chambers, and ran into culs-de-sac, fissures, and shafts. I constantly expected to reach the end of the cavern, but finding nothing, I was beginning to think uneasily of retreat when I saw a faint light around a corner. A broken and rising tunnel brought me to an undiscovered opening, a loophole in the cliff at whose foot the Rio de la Valleta runs.

The way the cavern had been formed was plain. It had once been an underground diversion of the river; a part of the torrent had gone in by the loophole, passed down through the heart of the mountain, and had come out in a waterfall from the mouth of the cavern to the river-bed. It was an exact natural counterpart of the channels dug parallel to mountain torrents to feed power-plants.

The course of nature transformed the Escaleta cavern; the river wore down its bed, and the upper loophole got beyond reach of freshets. In the words of É.-A. Martel, describing a similar phenomenon, the cavern became 'a fossil fragment of a river.'

The seven shafts of varying depth in the main gallery represent seven outlets of the water, which had obeyed Martel's 'law of oubliettes', tirelessly digging, going ever downward. The stream had dug out a lower level under the cavern; a torrent rumbled there, but so far it was out of my reach, the shafts being either too narrow or blocked with clay and gravel.

The Rio de la Valleta rushes tumultuously past the cliff between the two outer openings of the grotto. I went downstream, wading and leaping from block to block, and discovered that the perpendicular limestone cliff was full of fissures and conduits where the water passed, now in, now out. One of these tunnels, three feet above the water-line, let me into the cliff again. The passage descended gently, ending in a narrow crack blocked by a heap of rocks, through which I plainly heard the same roar that reached the upper level of the cavern.

For the second time that day I went at the rough job of sapping and mining by hand. Finally I slipped into a narrow gut along which ran a swift, icy stream. To my no little astonishment the current did not come from the Valleta torrent, but went towards it. This was, then, an underground tributary which would rise in the very bed of the river.

Clinging to rock projections, bracing arms and legs between the walls, sometimes getting into the water, I soon reached the cascade whose roar, now deafening, had guided me. A few yards upstream a narrow vertical chimney rose towards the upper level; the water came from a deep well, evidently the lower arm of a siphon which stopped further exploration.

The Escaleta cavern held no further secrets, so at sundown I went back across the Plan Ayguallud, and lay down to sleep under a granite block near a corral just abandoned by the flocks; their bells tinkled long through the dusk from the direction of La Rencluse. The Trou du Toro cataract roared at my feet; I overlooked the whole dried lake-bottom of the Ayguallud plain, and saw the border ridge between Aragon and Catalonia, and the Maladetta, the Accursed Mountains.

The sun flamed its last, and disappeared over the dome of Néthou. From under my boulder I watched the night come on. The moon rose oddly in the notch of the Pic de la Fourcanade; all night its pale light bathed ridges and slopes, sparkling on the streams of the Plan Ayguallud, stilled by the nocturnal frost. The wan glow even reached my stone lean-to.

My sleep was necessarily broken by gymnastic efforts to get warm. The discomforts of sleeping outdoors at 6,500 feet in wet rags of clothes, with nothing to eat but bread and cheese, are no doubt considerable, but I have always found the thrill of the high mountains more than worth it.

At five a.m. I left my precarious shelter, recrossed the Plan Ayguallud, and made a few more observations at the cavern of the Escaleta. Then I went up the Rio de la Valleta toward the end of the high valley, closed by the Mulieres peak and glacier. Here the torrent flows through a gorge of curious geological formation. The bottom is a narrow band of limestone, pinched between the granite strata of the peak of the Barrancos and the schist slope of Mount Pumero. Landslips from the latter block the river-bed, their rust colour standing out against the white limestone.

A thousand feet upstream from the Escaleta cavern the Rio de la Valleta rises abundantly from schist landslip which completely obstructs the bed; above this the bed is dry, and hardly visible.

From the little cliff of the right bank, where the heap of debris was piled up, I scanned the resurgence. It was impenetrable, and I thought it abnormal. Descending to the river-bed, I soon found a small, black hole at the foot of the limestone wall; I crawled in at once, and was quickly in a large tunnel with a torrent rushing down. Upstream it was too dark to see more than fifteen or twenty yards; downstream the tunnel narrowed abruptly, to pour its water through the impenetrable resurgence I had just seen.

It was only eight a.m., yet I did not have time that day to finish studying the new cavern. I struggled upstream by candlelight, clinging to the wet, polished rock sides of the river. Now wading or walking on the stone banks, now stretching out in flat tunnels, now crawling under long stretches of low ceiling, now climbing to higher levels, I pushed nearer and nearer the source of the river. As I went I counted six openings in the ceiling, each showing a bit of blue sky or a flicker of daylight.

There was a specially rugged stretch where the torrent cascaded and bellowed; beyond, I found a siphon, with deep, calm water coming from under a submerged vaulting. But this was not the end of the cavern. Climbing around the walls, I found in an upper level a maze of galleries that criss-crossed, wove over and under one another, and ended in impasses, with the roar of the cascades beyond. The falls were near, but upstream from the siphon, and thus inaccessible.

On my way back I needed all my nerve to combat doubts of direction at the various forks. I did find my way back to the guiding river-bed, but only to see that the water was rising. The glaciers were so near that the daily thaw in fine weather caused a regular freshet. I could not help thinking of the twenty-five-foot rise in the level of the Trou du Toro which I had noticed between four in the morning and five at night.

I got out of the cavern late, slept a few hours on the spot, and spent the rest of the night going on with the exploration in safety (so far as freshets were concerned). I ventured into narrow conduits whose ceilings still dripped with the forced draught of the day. The sun was already high when I came shivering from the cavern. I had crawled, climbed, and waded two-thirds of a mile, and reached the end of the cavern, but had not found the source of the torrent. To this I now turned my attention, despite great fatigue and the near-exhaustion of my provender.

Far up the valley, at the foot of the Pic de la Fourcanade, I saw a foaming torrent which I thought must be the same I had been exploring underground. I went in that direction. As I expected, I found at the end of a dried lake-bottom a place where the Rio de la Valleta totally vanished through two impenetrable apertures.

Only a few yards off was a long, rugged corridor carved out of immaculately white crystalline limestone, and pierced by oubliettes. Nearby a cavern mouth let me into the upstream part of the cavern, where I found the torrent underground again.

This last exploration I began by day, and at night pursued into recesses flooded by the daily freshet. I found a complicated system of galleries, three of which, containing running water, converged in a rotunda chamber; in the chamber was a chasm which led off the combined waters to reappear downstream at the siphon already described. The two caverns are really but one. As they lie between the Trou du Toro and the pass of the same name, I baptized them with the joint name of Grotte du Toro.

A year later (July 1929) I came back with my wife, and we discovered the narrow aperture of a natural well. This sixty-five-foot shaft gave on to a horizontal gallery of 650 feet long, leading to communication with the Grotte du Toro. The gallery is crossed by another, containing a deep stream which joins underground with the torrent in the Toro cavern. The new discovery brought the extent of this curious and dangerous cavern to 4,900 feet.

THE TRUE SOURCE OF THE GARONNE

*

ONE day at school, when I was about eight, we had for our geography lesson 'The Garonne and its Tributaries.' My class-mates stood up one after another to repeat in a rapid monotone: 'The Garonne rises in Spain at the foot of the Val d'Aran.'

I got up in my turn, and I can still hear the giggles that greeted my opening sentence: 'The Garonne rises in Spain among the glaciers of the Monte Maladetta.' The teacher stopped me to ask what book I had learned the lesson from. I had to confess that I had preferred an old geography full of pictures to our own dry school-book.

Our kind old teacher smilingly explained that geographers had changed their minds. The former ascription of the Garonne to the Monte Maladetta was a mistake. He also took occasion to tell us what a delicate matter it sometimes was to find a stream's true source; he cited, among others, the Nile, whose rise was still mysterious.

I should have been the last to imagine that a quarter-century later I should answer the ancient riddle of the Garonne.

Since my childhood the sources of the Nile have ceased to be a puzzle, as have the tributaries of Lake Victoria Nyanza, and it is strange but true that the great river of the Pyrenees was the last of the three to be fully explored.

Before embarking on a tangled subject, I may remark that I was not trying to solve a mere matter of local geography, theoretical and limited in interest. The object of my three years' work was a geographical, geological, and hydraulic problem of the first order, with important economic and political results.

There is only one Garonne in France, but in Spain there are several *garonas* (the general name for torrents in the Spanish

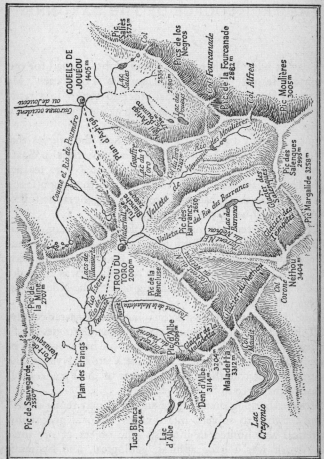

The Region in which the Garonne rises. The dotted line shows the underground course of the Garonne

central Pyrenees) tributary to the great French river. The Garonne results from the union in the Val d'Aran of two main streams, the Garona of the Val d'Aran, or eastern branch, and the Garona of Jouéou, or western branch.

Geographically, the Val d'Aran belongs to France: it is on the north slope of the Pyrenees, and its easy communication with France and inaccessibility from the rest of Spain would logically justify its annexation. It has been French and Spanish by turns, the plaything of conquest, treaties, and matrimonial conventions; in 1808 it was given to France, presumably for the last time. But in the treaties of 1815 the Val d'Aran was forgotten, and thus reverted to Spain in the confusion.

Of the two *garonas*, the eastern rises at a tiny spring in the pastures of the Pla de Beret; the western at an abundant spring called the Goueil de Jouéou (Eye of Jupiter) at the bottom of the short Jouéou valley.

The insignificant rivulet of the Pla de Beret has long been called the source of the Garonne, but this hardly makes sense, for the Goueil de Jouéou is far more abundant. The real problem is the source of the torrent of Jouéou. It flows so plentifully that it has rightly been considered the resurgence of a stream from far up the mountain. Opinions on the origin of this stream have changed several times in the course of centuries, and debate has been sharp.

The resurgence called the Goueil de Jouéou is at the mouth of an amphitheatre of high mountains, the Cirque d'Artiga de Lin. It rises in the midst of the forest, among luxuriant vegetation, at an altitude of 4,580 feet. The water foams and thunders out of a heap of boulders into a 130-foot cascade.

Higher up, the Cirque d'Artiga de Lin contains several lakes with underground tributaries, and torrents which vanish and reappear in the most capricious fashion. It would seem natural to consider the Goueil de Jouéou the complete and final resurgence of the waters above.

All the writers and armchair geographers have, in fact, called the resurgence the origin of the Garonne. But they have forgotten or ignored the dispute begun in 1787 among geologists, cartographers, and explorers who have combed the region.

In the massif of the Monte Maladetta, near the Val d'Aran, but on the opposite slope of the Pyrenees, is the celebrated Trou du Toro (Hole of the Bull), so called from the roar of the water which pours in. The rushing torrent comes from the huge melting snow-field and from almost a hundred acres of glacier, as described in the preceding chapter. This engulfment is uncommonly imposing and peculiar, and has long fascinated travellers and native mountaineers – the more so because no one knew where the great water-spout reappeared. The abyss is at an altitude of 6,500 feet, in the heart of a chaotic and geologically complicated region.

There have been two principal theories to explain the riddle of the Trou du Toro. The first, and seemingly the most probable, was that the water reappeared further down the Esera valley in various ponds, resurgences, and torrents forming the Rio Esera, which joins the Ebro to flow to the Mediterranean.

The second theory was a bold one, which seemed to defy the laws of nature. Its proponents claimed that the waters of the Trou du Toro changed valley, basin, and slope, passing under the ridge of the Pyrenees and rising again at the Goueil de Jouéou in the Val d'Aran to form the western branch of the Garonne, a tributary of the Atlantic.

Starting with the celebrated naturalist Ramond, the most eminent travellers and men of science lined up behind the two theories; but no definite proof had been offered, despite the inconclusive experiments of Émile Belloc in 1897.

In 1928, as I have already told, I was looking for underground streams at high altitudes in the Maladetta, hoping incidentally to find another frozen cavern like the Grotte Casteret. Shivering with cold, I stood on the edge of the Trou du Toro one morning at four. I dreamed for a long time as I stood there, wondering whether the water that swirled at my feet flowed to the Atlantic or the Mediterranean. Suddenly I made up my mind to answer that question, cost what it might.

It was lucky that my resolve was a firm one; I was four years in finding the answer. I went at it without preconceived ideas, knowing only that the problem would be immensely complicated.

Personal exploration, my favourite method, was out of the question here: the Toro abyss is impenetrable, for the water goes down through a bed of shifting sand. A coloration test, on the other hand, was prohibitively expensive, so I had to search and explore patiently all the shafts, fissures, cavities, and caves of the region, in the hope that they would give me hints or would let me into the mysterious underground stream.

I thus discovered and explored many new pits and caverns. but none led where I wanted to go. I had to change my attack, and undertake a study of the massif's entire geology and hydrography. This study, in the fearfully broken and complicated terrain of the Maladetta, took three years. I worked at all seasons; my days were often tedious, sometimes dangerous, always exhausting. I noted and followed the tiniest trickles, comparing flow, high and low water, deposits, and temperature of the torrents, their disappearances and resurgences. I let nothing escape me. I went even to spots where no guide or chamois-hunter had preceded me.

I shall not go into the tedious technical details of my enormous task; let me say simply that I divided it into four parts, to which I devoted four separate campaigns.

In 1928 I undertook to chart the hydrography of the upper slope of the Trou du Toro basin. I wanted to learn the exact origin, course, and hydraulic possibilities of the two chief torrents which joined to vanish in the Trou du Toro. This campaign I carried on in a vast mountain amphitheatre including such celebrated peaks as the Fourcanade, the Pic des Tempêtes, Néthou, the Coronado, and Maladetta. I learned that the Rio de los Barrancos and the Rio de las Mulieres and their tributaries, which feed the Trou du Toro, came from the melting of great frozen snow-fields and from five glaciers. The Mulieres torrent was surprising and difficult; at 7,150 feet it plunges underground, and I had to wade in water at thirty-nine degrees Fahrenheit through nearly a mile of rugged galleries.

In 1929 I went at the second item on the programme, the

hydrography of the Esera valley, which lies next to the Trou du Toro region. I followed the valley of the Rio Esera as far as the little town of Venasque, fifteen and a half miles from the Trou du Toro. This lovely valley, which divides the Haute-Garonne department from the Maladetta massif, contains a complex series of disappearances, resurgences, intermittent ponds, and overflows – a series which had given rise to the belief that the various resurgences were fed by the Trou du Toro. By long observation I disentangled the streams, and determined that the water of the Trou du Toro does not reappear in the Esera valley. I was lucky enough to find the real source of the Esera, which had never been exactly located.

In 1930 I left the Monte Maladetta and the southern slope of the Pyrenees, to work in the Cirque d'Artiga de Lin above the Goueil de Jouéou on the north slope. The steep amphitheatre is scored with deep ravines, and I discovered that its topography has never been more than roughly sketched. Here I found lakes, ponds, chasms that absorbed water, and torrents which skipped in and out of the ground in extraordinary fashion. Exploring their underground course was a real adventure. My 1930 campaign was the most strenuous of the four, but it was highly instructive. I proved to my own satisfaction that the streams of the Cirque d'Artiga did not feed the Goueil de Jouéou.

By 1930 I knew, therefore, that the waters of the Trou du Toro did not reappear in the Esera valley, and that the source of the Goueil de Jouéou was not in the Cirque d'Artiga de Lin.

The answer was almost evident.

At the same time there was one other theory, improbable but still possible. The Goueil de Jouéou might have an unknown source other than the Trou du Toro, and the Trou du Toro might have no resurgence, but might empty into the bowels of the earth.

Checking up on this theory was the fourth part of my programme. I studied the intervening and neighbouring basins, the high valleys of the Salenques, the Ribagorzana, Malibierne, and the Rio Negro, and found some interesting hydro-geological phenomena. But they had nothing to do with my problem.

This last investigation disposed of all doubts. I had attacked the question backward, gathering negative proof, but in the course of three years I had also collected a number of strong hydro-geological arguments favouring communication between the Bull and Jupiter's Eye. These arguments are too technical for the present book, but taken together with my actual discoveries they made a plain case for the connexion I claimed. I published the study as a long memoir in the bulletin of the Toulouse Natural History Society, concluding that the torrent swallowed in the Trou du Toro reappeared at the Goueil de Jouéou after passing two and a half miles through the ridge of the Pyrenees, and that the main source of the Garonne was therefore on the south slope of the Monte Maladetta.

I also mentioned the alarming fact that a Spanish power project was planned to divert the waters of the Trou du Toro for a large plant in the Esera valley. The power company saw no obstacles in its path, since it planned to return the water to the Esera valley, where the stream was thought to emerge in any case.

Here I stepped in; convinced as I was that the stream went north and not south, I trembled for the Garonne. The Spanish project would have dried up the Goueil de Jouéou almost entirely, diminishing the flow of the Garonne by half where it entered France. I was sure that the building of the plant would have irreparable consequences in the upper valley and along the plains of the Garonne.

Offering to prove my theory experimentally, I asked funds for a costly coloration test.

In vain.

Then I sent a detailed report to the governmental authorities. I laid aside my pick, dulled by three years' hard service, and put down my pen with a sigh of satisfaction, thinking my task was over.

Alas, the answer was slow in coming, and decisions were

slower still. Months passed, and there was no sign of improvement in an alarming situation. The sword of Damocles hung by an ever slenderer thread. From the high ridges I watched in helpless distress while the preliminary staking and levelling of the Esera valley went on. The Spanish project was becoming a reality. I learned that the Ebro Power Company had raised the capital necessary for the great undertaking of diverting the Garonne, and the catastrophe was imminent.

I returned to the charge with one last effort. Although the problem of the source of the Garonne was traditionally insoluble by scientific deduction, several eminent men were convinced by my arguments and by the impending danger to the Garonne. Among the most important were Camille Jullian, of the Académie Française, Alfred Lacroix, permanent secretary of the Academy of Sciences, and Monsieur Martel, the highest authority on subterranean hydrology. They had taken an interest in my previous work, and they thought the time ripe for a final concrete answer to the argument.

Thanks to them I was able to make good my previous offer, which had been far too expensive for my own pocket. A costly coloration test would make my conclusions public and indisputable, and give grounds for opposing the Spanish project, by recourse to international law if necessary.

There were subventions from the Academy of Sciences, the Institute of Hydrology, the General Council of the Haute-Garonne, and the Société du Puits de Padirac; to these I added the amount of the Prix Martel, which had just been awarded me by the French Geographical Society. Together, they were enough to buy the huge quantity of fluorescein necessary for the experiment.

An observer near the Trou du Toro, in the heart of the Accursed Mountains, on 19 July 1931, would have been much puzzled by the doings of five persons who were busy rolling kegs along the brink of the cliffs. A carabineer might have thought they were smugglers hiding their contraband; but it was only my party getting ready for the coloration test.

The party consisted of my mother, my wife, two friends of

theirs, Mlle Casse and Mlle de Sède, myself, and a Spaniard with a mule. We had left Luchon at dawn, and crossed the boundary ridge at the Port de Vénasque, finally arriving at the Trou du Toro. The mule carried six metal barrels, each containing twenty pounds of fluorescein, the most powerful colouring agent known. We unloaded them, and the mule and its master departed for the nearest village, twelve miles away.

We were left crouching against great boulders out of the way of a fierce cold wind, facing the Accursed Mountains; we could see the glaciers close at hand, and the jagged ridge, never lower than 10,400 feet. I explained the steps in the coloration test to Mlles Casse and de Sède, valiant young girls who had defied the mountain, and were ready to sleep on the bare ground if the expedition required it.

The celebrated Pyreneist Pierre Soubiron, in his guide book, describes the Trou du Toro as 'one of the curiosities of the Maladetta region. Situated at an altitude of 6,565 feet, it is a round, very regular, and very deep basin, into which falls a lovely cascade from the glaciers of Néthou, the Salenques, and the Mulieres. It is completely surrounded by abrupt walls, where we look down on the tranquil waters of the lake from a great height.'

Evening descended with alternating cloud rifts and dark threats. Processions of mist and tangled fog masked and unmasked the glaciers, where we watched the upward march of the sunny zone. The last flames of sunset clung to Néthou's dome, flashed for a moment on the summit among the eternal snows, and then vanished. Night, already drowning the valleys, rose to attack the peaks.

Sunlight affects fluorescein, which we could therefore not throw in until twilight; it must lose none of its properties before starting on its mysterious journey.

I gave the eagerly awaited signal. We had already arranged a code, because all conversation would shortly be impossible in the roar of the cataract. My wife and I crouched at the top of the cascade, with the open kegs in easy reach. We began to toss out the fluorescein, which would be completely dissolved and stirred up by the fall of the torrent. The other three members of the party stationed themselves at intervals to watch the narrow, roaring 500-foot gully which began at the bottom of the cascade and ran down to the pool.

From the first cask I scooped up a fine, almost impalpable brown powder, which I flung into the torrent. A magnificent colour overspread the cascade with the suddenness of an explosion; a few handfuls made it a green waterspout, fluorescent and indescribable. The gorgeous flood bounded tempestuously down the gully to the Trou; our companions, as enthusiastic as we, waved and gesticulated toward the cliff-tops.

For three-quarters of an hour we kept up our sowing gestures, but we never got used to the result. The extravagant and unreal colour of the torrent lent the whole countryside a truly diabolical look. We threw down the iron casks to make sure of using the last precious bit of powder, and then we hurried toward the Trou du Toro. A triple burst of laughter greeted us: my wife and I had powdered each other thoroughly with fluorescein as we worked, and we were brown from head to foot except where moist lips and eyes had turned green.

We cared for nothing but the Trou, a huge, round, deep paint-pot with smooth, vertical walls. The new clear torrent did not seem to dilute the extraordinary colour.

Darkness tore us from the magic view. Shelters are scarce in the Pyrenees, and it was time to hunt up a place for the night. I led my party five hundred yards down the valley to a miserable stone hut which had never known such splendour. We huddled in a litter of musty pine needles. All of us shrivelled, trying to forget our discomfort in slumber, but we were in for a bad night; the cold was piercing.

I could think of nothing but our experiment; in vain I tried to distract myself. I remembered the day, already long past, when I had first come to look at the Trou du Toro, and had slept, lulled by the roar of the cascade, under a boulder. But to-day the eternal, monotonous bellow that disturbed the night brought back too many memories and too many puzzles to let me sleep.

For three years I had not passed a day without asking myself,

'Where does that stream go?' Now, during that endless night, I knew the magic colour was on its way through the labyrinths of the Maladetta; in spirit I was scrambling through gigantic clefts. The underground torrent would be roaring in its stony prison at this very moment, passing two-thirds of a mile deep under the ridge between Aragon and Catalonia, to rise in the Goueil de Jouéou. Surely, objectively, implacably, the colour would give the long-sought answer.

At four a.m. we were all up, snorting in the chill blackness. We plodded up to the Trou du Toro under a heavy, threatening sky. From the cliffs we scanned the crater, which looked sinister at dawn. The water was clear again; all the colour had gone underground.

This important point determined, we exchanged final instructions, and the party split up. My wife and her two friends, the 'Esera detachment', went down the valley of that name to watch the tangle of disappearances and resurgences where the stream rose to pour into the Mediterranean.

As I watched them go, bent double under their knapsacks, I could not help admiring the two girls, who had bravely accompanied my wife alone in the high mountains on a hard and tedious job of uncertain duration. I feel I must thank them here for an unselfish enthusiasm, the more remarkable because we found it in none of the other young people whom we had hoped to enlist in our mission.

Thus assured that the Rio Esera would be well taken care of, the 'Garonne detachment' (my mother and I) set out from the Accursed Mountains to cross the ridge between Aragon and Catalonia, and stand sentry at the Eye of Jupiter. We crossed the Plan Ayguallud, and went up the Mulieres valley, which I had explored three years before; on the Col du Toro we were assaulted by a tempest of wind, rain, and fog. The steep northern slopes of this pass, which dominates the Cirque de Jouéou, demand close attention to business from climbers. Going down the precipice in the thick of the fog was a ticklish matter, but we could not put off our visit to the Goueil, so we started down the pitch. We descended 1,950 feet, treading the bottom of the amphitheatre with relief at last.

We were soaked through with fog and rain, which now redoubled their fury; I was covered from head to foot with fluorescein, and the water turned me into a dripping statue of blazing green!

For three years I had crossed and re-crossed that amphitheatre. But the storm was so thick that we could not get our bearings, and we had to cross the pastures of Artiga de Lin by compass. Finally we stumbled on a shepherd's hut, which I knew well, but had despaired of finding. On the hearthstone we saw a small bundle of faggots, which we kindled at once. Our knapsacks were in a sad state from the rain, and we had to dry everything out.

While my mother was doing this, I took advantage of a lull to visit the Goueil. I soon sighted the edge of the Jouéou forest, in the midst of which hides the great resurgence, one of the largest in Europe. Its tremendous roar betrays it from afar, and I steered toward it by the noise.

I hardly imagined that the colour would have got through the mountain yet. Underground waters usually move very slowly; they meander, and are held up by spillways, cave-ins, filtering sand-banks, and other obstacles. Underground lakes, enormous pockets, often retard the circulation still further. Uneasily I remembered coloration tests where the fluorescein had not reappeared for a week, a fortnight, twenty days. How were we to stay so long in the high mountains, with our one blanket and a few days' rations?

I rushed feverishly toward the cascade, which was still hidden behind beeches and firs. Suddenly I saw through the leaves a part of the resurgence.

I stood rooted to the spot. The cataract pouring from the mountain was a vivid green! I rushed up to get a better view; I feasted my eyes; my head whirled with memories.

The Garonne *did* rise in the Maladetta.

For a moment I was too excited to know how I felt; then I remember laughing aloud. I hurried back to the cabin to tell the good news to my mother, who was fixing up the place for a long stay. In a twinkling, everything was back in our wet knapsacks, the fire was out, the door closed; we said a cheerful good-bye to the hovel, congratulating ourselves on escaping long hours in the smoky lair.

We were soon standing in the spray and noise of the cascade, greedily admiring the brilliant green. The experiment was as good as finished, but we had still to find witnesses who would sign affidavits to prove it. We started down the Garonne in search of our first witnesses.

According to the figures (120 pounds of fluorescein will colour 528,000,000 gallons perceptibly to the naked eye), the colour was bound to go on down the Val d'Aran into France.

For an hour we went through the forest, down the valley, enjoying our rare glimpses of the emerald flood. Beyond the forest, where the fields began, two reapers stopped their work as we came by, and rushed up to ask if we had seen the Garonne. They had seen the '*diabolica*' colour that morning at six, when they got up; they had kept going over to watch the colour ever since.

I explained the phenomenon, reassured them, and got them to sign the first of many witnesses' statements. One of them had believed 'that a sulphur mine had burst in the mountain'; the other was very uneasy about the trout.

Almost every one seemed to think the trout would be exterminated, so intense was the colour. No matter how much I insisted that fluorescein was absolutely harmless, some people did not believe me; but even the most incredulous had to admit they had seen no dead fish.

We hurried on down the valley to get to the wretched Ermitage d'Artiga de Lin, where we hoped to rest, dry out, and refresh ourselves; but that day was fated to give us no respite. In the kitchen an old woman bustled about getting coffee, explaining excitedly that the colour of the river was 'a miracle of the fairies, and must mean that something terrible was going to happen.' I went to the window, looking out over the valley. While I was trying to see how far the colouring went on, I noticed in the distance two carabineers hurrying toward the Ermitage. Undoubtedly they too believed in the river-poisoners' misdeeds, and they were rushing from the village of Las Bordas to pursue the poachers.

My green clothes, face, and hands accused me beyond a doubt. I could explain as much as I pleased that I was no poacher, but a harmless experimenter; would they believe me? If not, the discussion might turn out badly for us.

Taking no chances, we forwent an oratorical contest, and left precipitately, to the blank astonishment of the innkeeper. Despite our growing fatigue and our heavy bags we walked fast up the valley. We repassed the Goueil, still as green as ever. To avoid the Col du Toro we re-entered Aragon by the monotonous, endless slopes of the Port de la Picade. We were worn out when we got there.

From the ridge we scrutinized the Esera through the glass; it wound away far below our feet, but there was no trace of colour.

We had now to go down the valley in search of the other detachment. We followed the meandering *rio* for a long time without finding a trace of our companions. At nightfall, after fourteen hours on foot, we found them encamped. Their astonishment at seeing us rise out of the darkness vied with their delight at the unexpected quick success of the coloration test.

Though we were impatient to go back and see how far the fluorescein had penetrated into the French Department of Haute-Garonne, we spent four days and four nights watching the Rio Esera, which never ceased to run clear.

We finished the last day by climbing the Maladetta pass and peak (10,764 feet). When we got back to France we learned from abundant testimony that the colour, intense in the Val d'Aran, had been clearly visible beyond Saint-Béat, thirty-one miles from the Trou du Toro.

The discovery was put on official record by a communication to the Academy of Sciences, and I strained every nerve to publicize it in an effort to rouse opinion and interest the authorities. At last I had the satisfaction of learning that they had become uneasy over the situation.

Not only would a Spanish diversion of the waters of the Trou du Toro halve the flow of the Garonne, but the western, or Jouéou, branch is the more important of the two branches because it comes from melting glaciers only. It thus becomes a compensating regulator. In the summer the streams of the Val d'Aran (whose basins have no glaciers) are largely dried up, and the Garona of Jouéou shows its superiority: the greater the drought and heat, the more the glaciers of the Maladetta melt, and the more water the Trou du Toro sends to the Goueil de Jouéou. Without this natural governor in dry seasons, the industry and agriculture of the upper Garonne would atrophy.

The time came for conversations with Spain; my role was over, and it was the turn of the ministers, the diplomats, and the residents of the Garonne. The question was delicate, for there seemed to be no exact precedent for international litigation over an underground watercourse.

Parliamentary and governmental action, supported by a vigorous newspaper campaign, seemed sure to produce a favourable outcome; the Spanish Republic could not but admit that the French claims were justified.

But the whirlpool in the Trou du Toro was nothing to the whirlpool of powerful private interests stirred up by the question of the Garonne, to the prejudice of the public interest; it was long before the Spanish Government yielded to the facts, and abandoned the power project.

INDEX